YOUNG VOICEWORKS

32 Songs for Young Singers

compiled and written by
Jo McNally

series editor: Peter Hunt

MUSIC DEPARTMENT

OXFORD
UNIVERSITY PRESS

OXFORD
UNIVERSITY PRESS

Great Clarendon Street, Oxford OX2 6DP, England
198 Madison Avenue, New York, NY, 10016, USA

Oxford University Press is a department of the University of Oxford.
It furthers the University's aim of excellence in research, scholarship,
and education by publishing worldwide in

Oxford   New York
Auckland   Cape Town   Hong Kong   Karachi
Kuala Lumpur   Madrid   Melbourne   Mexico City   Nairobi
New Delhi   Shanghai   Taipei   Toronto

With offices in

Argentina   Austria   Brazil   Chile   Czech Republic   France   Greece
Guatemala   Hungary   Italy   Japan   Poland   Portugal   Singapore
South Korea   Switzerland   Thailand   Turkey   Ukraine   Vietnam

Oxford is a registered trade mark of Oxford University Press
in the UK and in certain other countries

3 5 7 9 10 8 6 4 2

ISBN 978–0–19–343555–1

Music and text origination by
Barnes Music Engraving Ltd., East Sussex
Printed in Great Britain on acid-free paper by
Caligraving Ltd., Thetford, Norfolk

Illustrations by Philip Atkins

Preface

Young Voiceworks is a collection of songs and vocal activities designed to help young singers and their leaders develop healthy voices for a lifetime of singing and pleasurable music-making. The songs teach basic musical concepts for primary-aged children and make up a 'working repertoire' that can be revisited throughout the primary school years. The songs are short, fun to sing, and accessible. Teachers and singing leaders at all stages will find these songs a useful addition to their concert programmes and music curriculum.

When I began to teach in international schools for the first time, my classes included students from over twenty five different nationalities. Embracing the diversity of this worldwide perspective was a challenge that shaped my thoughts and practice of music education. Working in the UK at both public and private schools helped me to extend this into a series of materials that would be useful for both the specialist and the non-specialist music teacher.

Young singers aged 5–7 (key stage 1) are a unique group. At the lower end of this age group will be children who have experienced playgroup and nursery classes, but there will be many others who are totally new to school, with its scheduled day and the challenge of working within a larger group of individuals. Some children will speak clearly, and some will still be struggling to communicate. In our multi-ethnic communities some children will speak English as a second language, while for others it might be a totally new experience. All these communities bring something to our joint culture, and music—especially singing—is a bridge to that communication. Experiencing music from other cultures helps children from diverse backgrounds to share and bond, and brings an exciting opportunity to 'taste and feel' the language and sound of another culture.

These days few families regularly sing at home. Much of what we think of as 'children's songs' is suitable only for listening to or for fun, and is not appropriate for developing young voices. It's not so much a question of range as of the difficulty of the melodic line. By using simple and accessible songs, young singers will be engaged and successful in making music from the start of each session.

Each song in *Young Voiceworks* prepares and reinforces basic concepts. The songs are meant to become part of a 'working repertoire' that will be a basis for continuing development throughout the primary years and beyond. A working repertoire is a start; it's meant to be added to. As you explore the songs and activities you'll become aware of how other materials—favourite or new songs, poems, texts, or games—may fit into each section. Add them, share them with your colleagues, and make them part of the pack you send on with your classes as they progress!

Acknowledgements

Teaching, learning to teach, and learning to learn doesn't just happen in a classroom. Teachers, mentors, colleagues, students, friends, and everyone you come into contact with adds to the 'mix' of who you are and how you work. I've been lucky and have had a great deal of support and encouragement, especially in the development of this book.

Firstly, thanks to Peter Hunt for developing Voiceworks and the Voiceworks 'style', which is such a great model to work from. Next, thanks to the folks at OUP—including Alistair Henderson, David Blackwell, Kristen Thorner, and Emily Chelu—who have guided and supported with the patience of saints during the production of this book. Thanks also to Ralph Woodward for his help with some of the piano accompaniments. Grateful appreciation goes to my colleagues Therees Hibbard, Peter Broadbent, Geoff Boyd, Rick Hein, Anne Torrent, Sheena Mason, Paul Ayers, Fran Carpenter, Phillip Stannard, and Hillingdon Music Service and Arts for Schools (Harrow), who by model and friendship add immeasurably to my life and work.

Special gratitude to all the singers/students who enrich my life daily, especially to Anne Lyons and the staff and students of St John Fisher School, who gave their time and support to the recording and development of these materials.

Finally to Chris, the most supportive partner one could wish for!

JO MCNALLY

Contents

Using Young Voiceworks

This book divides into the following sections:

Section I: Move that Voice. Finger plays, clapping games, and movement and dance. These songs get the voice, body, and mind active and ready to learn. They have a limited vocal range, lots of repetition, and tunes that are easy to remember. A great way to begin a lesson.

Section II: Keep the Beat. This section works towards keeping a steady pulse and learning about rhythm, one of the first steps in musical development. Question and answer songs, songs that layer rhythmic text, and simple rounds reinforce these skills.

Section III: The Singing Voice. Group songs exploring vocal range and an introduction to part singing. We'll explore slightly longer pieces and give opportunities for small group descants and some solo singing. There are also songs to develop confidence, as students learn to 'match pitch' and take control of their voices to sing beautifully.

Section IV: Songs from Many Cultures. Songs from around the world, each with an accessible text in its original language. Among other short songs, a Hindi song about the moon and a Japanese song about fireflies give a flavour of other cultures and their musical styles.

Section V: Just for Fun. New ways with old favourites and new songs to become favourites, not particularly for performance, just to be enjoyed any time!

Each song is headed with the relevant CD track number and accompanied by supporting text notes designed to help you teach and perform the material. The layout for each song is identical:

- **Information.** This section gives some history or brief background information to the piece, to give its context. It also introduces any key musical features.
- **Starting and teaching.** Suggestions for preparing to sing the piece, and a step-by-step guide showing how to teach the songs and how best to facilitate effective learning.
- **Ideas.** Extension ideas for taking the music further and developing the confidence and abilities of the singers.
- **Listen out.** Troubleshooting: a short list of problems that may arise, how to listen out for them, and how to prevent or correct them.
- **Performing.** Suggestions and ideas for performing the songs.

Getting started: thoughts on developing a working repertoire

The key to building a successful working repertoire is being aware of the needs of your group. There are many ways in which a song can be taught, developed, and performed. The teaching notes that accompany each piece give a range of options, but don't be limited to these. Try out your own ideas, and adapt these for the songs, games, and texts you currently use. Consider the following when choosing and teaching the songs in this book and in all your singing.

- *Be aware of why you choose a particular song to teach.*
  - Choose repertoire firstly because you like it. If you like it, so will your group (eventually!).
  - Think about what concept it can help to teach or reinforce.
  - Is the song useful for a special event or holiday programme?
- *Be aware of the basic structure of the song.*
- *What is the range of the song (how high/low is it)? Is it appropriate for your group, or does it need to be adapted?*
  - Are there any phrases or sections that repeat? Repetitions are great for gaining confidence quickly: they're easily recognizable, and your singers will remember them first. This is also true (to a lesser extent) of words that rhyme. Look for them!
  - Does the rhythm follow the words naturally, or is it imposed? It is easier to remember rhythms that follow the natural rhythm of the words, as in poetry and nursery rhymes. This doesn't mean that you should only use words that rhyme—just be aware.
  - Is the text appropriate for your singers?
- *How will you teach this song?*
  - Rote-singing and echoing will probably be the most appropriate way to begin.
  - Try introducing the text first.
  - Teach the rhythms by echo-clapping or reading rhythm cards (see p. xviii).
  - Listen to the CD, or sing the song to your group and ask them to identify how many phrases there are. Are any the same or different?
  - Have your group look at the score of the piece.
  - Could this song be introduced by someone 'special' (a student, another member of staff, visiting parent, grandparent, local musician, etc.)?
- *Look for ways the song can be extended.*
  - Change the key, moving the starting pitch higher or lower.
  - Change the dynamics (how loudly or quietly a song is sung).
  - Try the song at a different tempo, making it faster or slower.
  - Do the piece in canon, with one group starting before another.
  - Repeat a phrase as a rhythmic or melodic ostinato. This can be sung or transferred to instruments to add depth and length to any piece.
  - Add movement—anything from keeping a simple pulse to full-fledged choreography.
  - Add a game. There are suggestions throughout the book, but don't be limited by these: make up a game, or get your group to develop their own. Transfer the rhythm and/or melody to pitched or non-pitched percussion instruments.
  - Inner-hear part of the song to develop internal listening skills.
- *Reinforce good practice.*
  - Assume you and your group can do the work together musically!
  - Use your ears and improve the singing by asking for specifics. Listen to each other, sing with clear diction, check posture, and ask your group what they think and what they could change.
  - In every busy day, sing something!—not just for assigned music time, but every day. Sing a song as you change from one subject lesson to another, sing as you line up, sing as you wait for lunch, sing as you walk together on a field trip, sing as you are getting ready to go home ... just sing!
- *Look for and encourage the unexpected.*
  - No one knows everything and everyone has at least one interesting idea to contribute. Trust your instincts and don't worry if you get something wrong. I get things wrong all the time. It usually means I've skipped a step, or maybe something just doesn't work at a given moment. It may work another day, so I just re-group and try again, and so do my singers.
- *Singing is supposed to be fun, even for you!*

○ You don't have to be a professional singer to lead the singing, but you are a professional 'user of voice'. Take care of your instrument and enjoy the sounds you make (in my car I am fabulous!). Instil respect for all the voices in your care, and remember to enjoy!
* *Repetition, repetition, repetition!*
  ○ Improve a phrase or idea by repeating it until it comes back as you want it.

▦ Accompaniments

Most of my teaching is unaccompanied; we just sing. When using any type of accompanying instrument I generally keep it minimal and make sure it enhances and supports the singing without overpowering it. Here are some of the main instruments I prefer and why.

Guitar

The guitar is great. Gentle strumming or picking supports the singing sound, and the tone quality works really well with voices. It's portable, and most songs are accessible with just a few chords. I use a classical/Spanish-style guitar, not just because of the 'softer' quality of the sound, but because the (nylon) strings are easier on my fingers. The acoustic guitar works just as well, though, and has a more 'edgy' sound with its metal strings.

Piano/keyboard

I use this sparingly and try not to play the melody too often but to use chords to support the sound and encourage my singers—even young ones—to take ownership of their music. Even if a piece suggests a piano accompaniment, I will generally teach it without the piano first. The timbre of voice to voice is much easier to listen to and copy from than the piano. When you do use piano, play musically and especially not too loudly. Louder playing doesn't necessarily mean that your group will listen more or improve. By sometimes holding back a bit you'll encourage them to listen not only to themselves but to each other.

Boomwhackers

If you are unfamiliar with these, they are pitched plastic tubes in different lengths that are played by striking them either on the floor or against something. I prefer them with the caps on, which lowers the pitch by an octave. They provide a means of keeping a pulse harmonically, and are fun, easy to use, and have an interesting timbre.

Incidental percussion

I have suggested a variety of percussion (tuned and untuned) instruments with these songs. Not every school, playgroup, or singing leader has access to a lot of percussion instruments, and although it's nice and useful to have plenty, you don't need them. You can do lots with just a drum, tambourine, and triangle! Use what you have and feel free to change or experiment with any of the arrangements to suit what's available.

▦ The CD

The recordings are for reference and are not specifically performances. They are meant particularly for anyone who isn't comfortable reading music, to help them learn the basic song. Listen to each recording several times, and I suggest you look at the music while listening. This can really help if you are new to or less confident in music-reading.

The performance options are sung by young singers. Although they should reflect good practice, they are not meant to be perfect or the only way to sing the song but are offered as a suggestion. Be surprised by your group and the ways they adapt songs to make them their own. Many of my best ideas come from something surprising a group does during the session. Be inspired by your singers!

Also, try getting your group to listen to a new song before or after learning it. This can be helpful not only when learning it but when adding a percussion or extra vocal line.

Performance

Whether a performance is formal (such as a holiday programme, end-of-year concert, or assembly) or informal (sharing with another class, or just singing for a visitor), it should have a sense of occasion. This is a time to help build not only concert behaviour and polite attention to other performers, but also a sense of pride in the group's own accomplishments, and to establish good performance habits. Encourage good posture, no fidgeting, alive and active facial expression, and concentration throughout the performance. Oh, and there's one more thing—don't forget to have fun!

Multicultural songs

Don't be put off by the text or foreign languages used in the section 'Songs from Many Cultures'. The texts are mostly phonetic, and there may well be someone nearby who can help with pronunciation. Start with the CD. Be aware that the sound of each language varies because of the way the lips, teeth, tongue, and mouth shape are used when speaking. This will also vary between regional dialects for the same reason, so sometimes a simple song will sound differently even within a radius of a few miles. The point is, have a go. The taste of languages can be delicious and enjoying the music of other cultures rewarding.

Revisiting for key stage 2 (ages 7–11)

As part of a working repertoire, most of these songs can be used throughout the 5–11 age group. Remember, this is all a process. It's enough to just sing and enjoy the songs, but as you revisit each song, add or reinforce a concept. Change the dynamics and vary the tempo; look more closely at rhythm patterns; continue aural training; and learn to sight-sing. The songs are simple and short by design, to aid both young singers and their leaders to learn and grow together musically.

Recommended reading

Camden Music Service: *World Song Project*. Copies available from Camden Music Service, The Medburn Centre, 136 Chalton Street, London, NW1 1RX, tel: 020 7974 4075, email: camdenmusic@camden.gov.uk.
Lois Choksy: *The Kodály Method 1* and *2* (Prentice Hall)
Paul E. Dennison and Gail E. Dennison: *Brain Gym* (Edu-Kinesthetics, Inc.)
Katalin Forrai: *Music in Preschool* (Corvina)
Jane Frazee and Kent Kreuter: *Discovering Orff: A Curriculum* (Schott)
Stephanie Martin and Lyn Darnley: *The Teaching Voice* (Whurr Publishers)
Arvida Steen: *Exploring Orff: A Teacher's Guide* (Schott)

Preparing to Sing

▣ Vocal development: it's a process thing

'OK, let's sing'—three words to strike terror into the hearts of anyone, any time, any place. Just utter those words and perfectly competent adults go weak, normally loud and boisterous teenagers become silent. I think 5–7-year-olds are excited by the sounds they make because they're still interested in exploring the delicious way sounds taste and feel, not to mention how they can delight or torture the adults around them! It's a process that lasts a lifetime.

Babies have an interesting array of sounds. Because the tongue takes up proportionally more space in the mouth at this age than at any other time in life, they have a variety of 'moist' sounds. They gurgle, fascinated by the sound and feel of blowing bubbles; they make toothless chomping noises; their laugh is whole bodied; and their cry is loud with a pitch range an operatic soprano would envy.

During the next few years, as features develop and the tongue becomes more manageable, children develop their language through copying the sounds around them. Visit any grocery store and you'll hear children persistently asking 'why?', saying 'no', and—my personal favourite—doing 'the scream', but often lost in a world of their own sound. Often in a sing-song voice, children like to repeat words that 'taste' good—bits of songs, commercials, machine noises, animal sounds, and the like. They mimic the world around them, delighting in each victory to make themselves understood.

At 5–7 they are ready to begin a more cognitive process of 'vocal possibilities' and, with language skills attached to understanding, real progress can now be made in singing skills. Remember, learning to sing and to match pitch will take as long as it takes, and it will be different for every student.

▣ Before you start

Before you start singing, consider time, space, and organization.

Time

Little and often for this age group is great. Don't assume that one 30–45-minute session per week will suffice. It's a start, but every group should sing every day, even if only for a couple of minutes—repetition is essential. You also need to be aware of concentration limits. Often two or three 15-minute sessions will accomplish more than one longer session.

Space

Vary the activities in any lesson, so that you use a combination of sitting, standing, standing in a circle, and moving around. This age group—actually, any age group—finds it a challenge to remain in the same position for too long. If I need a group to stand or sit for an extended period, I will get them to stand and jump ten or fifteen times just to give them a mental break and something physical to do before beginning the next activity. Scheduling is often a challenge in schools, but try to incorporate different spaces for your lessons. Some schools have specific music rooms, but often these are not very generous as spaces for movement. Try to occasionally book a larger space for singing and music time, such as a school hall, gymnasium, or even outside (weather permitting).

Organization

I tend to think of my lessons as a meal: appetizer, main course, and dessert. The appetizer is a short, fun exercise as an attention grabber, to get the group to concentrate and work together. The songs in 'Move that Voice' are all good appetizers. The main course generally works to reinforce a specific concept. This can apply to any of the sections this book, but particularly 'Keep the Beat', 'The Singing Voice', and 'Songs from Many Cultures'. The songs in 'Just for Fun' are for dessert—but only after we've finished the main course! This is a good time to let your group choose the song or activity, although you might want to narrow the choice by offering an either/or option. If your class space allows, keep a list of the songs your group has done as the list grows.

▨ Warm ups

A physical and vocal warm up should be done daily, if possible at the beginning of the day and perhaps just after lunch. Consider it a 'stretch' time, and it need not take longer than a couple of minutes. This will not only prepare your group for music-making but will help with the transition to any subject area. Think of it as clearing a space and resetting for the next activity.

Physical warm ups

Posture and wake up. Before you begin and during an activity repeatedly check posture, yours and theirs. Good posture promotes a healthy singing sound. You are your instrument, and young singers have bodies that seem to grow and change almost daily. Here's the basics, which apply whether standing or sitting.

The body should feel 'tall and proud'. If you stand with your back against a wall, you'll feel your body move into place; then walk away keeping the same feeling. Walk away regally 'as a king or queen', or see the difference when you say 'be 3 inches/7 cm taller', but watch that the shoulders don't rise up as they can sometimes have a life of their own. If this happens, just raise them up and bring them back down several times to release and relax them. Remember to keep the feeling of standing tall and proud. Don't be manic about posture; just be observant and reinforce when good. Then choose from the following:

- **Take a shower**—well, an imaginary one. Give yourself a good 'scrub' from head to toes, then from toes to head. Don't forget to spend extra time on head and hair, and especially behind the ears.
- **Shake out that body**. Call out a body part and shake it. This can be the whole body or fine-tuned to smaller areas—the top half, bottom half, shoulders, arms, hands, fingers, legs, feet, toes.
- **Stretch**—just stretch everything! The key here is to hold each stretch for several seconds, enjoying the contrast between tension and relaxation.
- **Scrunch**. Scrunch up the face as tightly as possible and then release, opening the face as wide as possible, several times. If you're brave, add a sound as the face opens.
- **Mirror me**. Hide your face behind your hands and make a face (strange and weird faces work well). As you take away your hands, the group should mirror your look. This is a great game for students to lead.

- **Extend 'mirror me'.** Everyone hides their face behind their hands. Call out an emotion—happy, sad, excited, angry, surprised—and then get everyone to make the appropriate face at the same time.
- **Scary eyes.** Look up, look down, look to one side, look to the other side, make a circle one way and then the other. The eyes are often forgotten, although we use them constantly each day. This little extra 'stretch' makes you feel more alert and is great to use between lessons.
- **Shoulder shapes.** Move the shoulders up (hold), then down (hold), forward (hold), then back (hold); circle both shoulders forwards, then both backwards, then do the same one shoulder at a time (a bit like swimming).

Breathing. Be aware of breathing but don't make a big thing of it. (After all, you're still alive so you must have the basic hang of it!) The main thing to watch out for is that the shoulders don't move violently up and down when taking a breath. Here are a few fun things to try:

- **Tummy balloon.** Lie on your back on the floor with your hands on your tummy. Breathe in (inhale) and your hands will rise; breathe out (exhale) and they will lower. If you lie on your back on the floor it's virtually impossible to breathe incorrectly. Also, it's easier for each child to focus on the activity (instead of on their neighbour) when lying on the floor, and the body is naturally more relaxed.
- **Balloon with a slow leak.** As an extension of the above, lie on your back and exhale on any of these sounds: *ss, ah, zz, ff*. Try to make the sound last for a slow count to 4. Use different kinds of air sounds, varying the amount of breath and using muscle control to maintain the sound consistently. As your group develops, extend the slow count to 6, 8, 10, and even 12.
- **Bubbles.** Using an ordinary bottle of bubbles with a wand, gently blow to make bubbles. I've never known a child (or adult!) that doesn't like to blow bubbles. It's fun, but it's also a great breath-control exercise. Practise making lots of bubbles with short breaths, or a large bubble with a constant controlled stream of air.

Vocal warm ups

Use vocal gymnastics to develop vocal control, clear diction, and expressive singing and speaking.

- **A to Z.** Say the alphabet and see how far you can get in one breath. Your class will want to do this exercise very quickly because it's fun. Try slowing it down and use a 'keyboard rhythm' (you know the ones—electronic keyboards with rhythm patterns the kids discover first!); it's also a good opportunity to locate where the tempo/speed button is and let that determine how fast you go.
- **Count that.** Try the above exercise with chains of numbers—sequential, even, odd, and, when your group is ready, beginning times tables.

Tongue-twisters. These are a wonderful way to exercise the lips, teeth, and tongue and to promote clear diction. Try varying the dynamics, tempo, and quality of sound. Here are a few to get you started:

- A big black bug bit a big black bear.
- Toy boat. Toy boat. Toy boat.
- Sam's shop stocks short spotted socks.
- Inchworms itching.
- Friendly Frank flips fine flapjacks.
- Fat frogs flying past fast.
- Flee from fog to fight flu fast!

'Seashore six' is a tongue-twister song about a day at the beach. The spoken 'counting bars' can be used as an ostinato if you want to do the piece in two parts.

Seashore six (CD track 1)

Words and music by
Jo McNally

one two three four five six

sea - shore six, six slick sticks, six sea - shells,

six slip-pery snails. Star-fish, sand, sea-weed swim-ming in the salt - y waves,

shi - ning sun is all a - round we're at the beach to - day.

The shape game

There are several 'shapes' that all schools use to move groups from one place to another and from one lesson to another: line, circle, parallel lines, two circles, and 'individual places' are most frequently used. I often begin a sound—*tt*, *sh*, *mm*, etc.—when a group enters my class; they join in and make the shape we'll begin the lesson with. It saves time and helps the group to focus from the start of each session. This game helps to teach those shapes and incorporates the concepts of sound with movement and silence with stopping. It helps to teach group cooperation and develop listening skills, and introduces 'silence' as a concept. This is a really excellent way to 'save voice' (leader/teacher) and make time in an already busy day to include a vocal workout and include singing.

This exercise works really well when you introduce each sound gradually. Do not try to introduce all five shapes on the same day!

Shape	Card	Suggested sound
line (lining up)		*tt*
circle		*sh*
parallel lines (partners)		*mm*
circles (two groups)		*bb*
individual places		*zz*

- The leader initiates a given sound and/or shows the relevant card. The group joins in, making the sound continuously until the shape is made, and then everyone stops and there should be silence. Make sure you wait for the silence; encourage it, and enjoy it. (Silence is a great sound. Trying to get 'quiet' from a group requires a lot of energy and is probably one of the most time-consuming activities in a school day. When in our days is there a total silence? There is always noise from somewhere, whether it's the breeze from outside or, if a group is quiet enough, the hum from the lights, or the class next door.)
- Gradually introduce the sounds for the 'shapes' in your day. The sounds given are only suggestions. Feel free to choose your own sounds, or even use a song! Short songs work best.
- 'Sound shapes' is a movement piece that can be introduced when several or all the sounds can be done efficiently by your group. Connect the shapes with silences between them. With younger students, this works well in smaller groups of not more than six.
- Extend this game by getting older groups to decide the order of the shapes. Divide into two groups. Each group works independently, working in canon with one starting before the other. (This is more of a key stage 2 extender, but it is great to hear the sounds overlapping as a two-part piece.)

The name game

This is a sound-exploration game with improvisation in a call-and-response style—a variation on 'leader calls a name and student responds'. Try using this game when taking the register or when learning the names of a new class. Consider using the options where the class echoes before the student responds, as this helps to keep the full group focused and will not take any longer than the single student response.

- Call and response: leader calls a name, and student responds 'here I am'.
- Call, echo, response: leader calls a name; class echoes the name; then student responds 'here I am'.
- Try calling the name in an interesting way. To extend this idea, ask the student to respond in the opposite way. The easiest ways to begin are loud/soft, high/low, and fast/slow.
- Stretch part of the name.
  - Stretch the beginning consonant or vowel: JJJJJJJJJJJJJJo *or* Joooooooooo
  - Stretch any part of the name: PPPPPPPeeeeeeeeettttttttter
- The student responds by exploring an interesting way to say/sing their name. The class should echo, repeating exactly.
  - Try a vocal shape, a direction or directions in combination:

This also works well as a steady pulse and movement game. Standing in a circle shape works well, but the game could also be done while seated in a normal class setting and is particularly useful when a group is just getting to know one other, as at the beginning of a new term.

- The first student says their name, and the group echoes. Try to keep this moving around the circle, but don't be too concerned about adding a steady pulse the first few times.
- Try adding a simple hand-clapping pattern, keeping it slow and steady:

- Practise saying your name in the empty space. To start with, everyone says their name at the same time, then take turns around the circle, each student saying their name in the next silent/empty space. Ideally, it should be the next silent space, but when learning it's more important to wait for any silent/empty space (rather than to say the name during the clapping).
- Again, explore interesting ways to say or repeat the names.
- As the name is said, try adding a physical movement such as a stamp or nod or shake of the head.
- A fun variation is to gradually speed up the pattern, perhaps incorporating not just first names but last names as well.

Vocal exploration

The voice is a creative and imaginative tool. Explore sounds working from simple known sounds such as animals (family pets, farm, zoo, imaginary), using the voice to imitate these sounds, and gradually combining them into 'sound stories' and 'soundscapes'. Gradually, the sound source can be increased to include machines, as well as natural sounds such as air/wind, water/waves, and the like. This is a good elementary compositional tool that can be revisited through all the key stages.

☐ Sound cards

What's the sound? Make cards of each of the following, using the samples below as starting sounds. Starting with animal noises and familiar items, show a card to your group and ask them to make the sound that goes with the picture. Then put the card down. When the picture is not showing, the sound should stop. (Silence.) Do this with each of the cards.

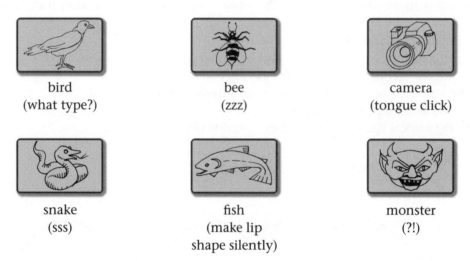

bird	bee	camera
(what type?)	(zzz)	(tongue click)

snake	fish	monster
(sss)	(make lip shape silently)	(?!)

- **Dynamics**. Try each card loud/quiet.
- **Directions**. Move the card up/down and ask your group if the sound is higher or lower. Now, all sounds can change pitch, but you're looking for the group effect and an obvious change. Don't be too picky about this; it's primarily an exercise connecting voice and listening skills.
- **Partner sounds**. Divide your group in two and show two cards—two sounds—simultaneously. Start/stop the sound on each side so you get variations of both sounds, one sound, and silence.
- **Sound sentence**. Organize the cards in a line of two or more (four cards make a good phrase length). Point to each card in turn to perform the piece. Extend this by deciding the duration of each sound (number of pulses for each card).
- **Animals**. Extend your repertoire of sounds by exploring animal noises. I don't mean just *woof*, *miaow*, *quack*, *moo*. Think about how they actually sound: large dogs sound different to small dogs, and angry cats sound different to purring cats.
- **Extra pictures**. If, like me, your artistic skills are questionable, take pictures from magazines or check your library for pictures and posters. Even better, get your group to make their own!

☐ Soundscapes and sound stories: developing listening skills

Developing listening skills can be a challenge. Children need something specific to listen for, instead of just listening randomly. Many schools have a 'composer of the week' or 'special music of the week' that plays while students arrive for an assembly. I suspect this music is never discussed after the fact (apologies where this isn't true). Consider asking the questions: what kind of emotions does it have? How does the music make you feel? Do you know any music or songs that have the same feeling? Is the music loud or quiet, or a combination of both? Are there many instruments or just a few? What type of instruments are being used? What type of group is playing? Who is singing (man, woman, old, young, child, a group for fun, a choir)?

Soundscapes give an opportunity to explore the 'real' sounds around you. There are the obvious sounds of events, such as a siren, that immediately focus our attention; and there are background sounds that can be as simple as the breeze. When both types of sounds are layered they give us an aural sense of place, a picture in sound. Here are two possibilities:

Day at the beach

Background sounds: waves, wind, occasional birds in the distance, dogs barking as they play.

Event sounds: walking on the sand (think about reactions if barefoot on hot sand), eating sounds (lunch), ice-cream seller, donkey rides.

In the cave

Background sounds: wind, water drops.

Event sounds: bats, echoing footsteps, rats, dragons.

- **School sounds.** Close your eyes and listen to your room; count the sounds you hear.
- **Sound walks.** Many schools do map-making projects. Why not add the sounds that may be heard along the way?
- **Sound stories.** As you listen to stories or tell stories to your group, make the background and event sounds that go with the story.

When exploring 'real' sounds, some of the best fun is in figuring out how to make the sounds and imitate them vocally.

- Think about the sound. Is it:
  - loud/quiet?
  - high/low?
  - near/far?
  - smooth/sharp?
  - short/long?
- How does the sound taste? Consider and explore:
  - the shape of the mouth: how open or closed is it?
  - the lip shape: are the lips used in making the sound?
  - the placement of the tongue: forward, back, roof of mouth, bottom of mouth?
  - breath: are you using a lot or a little?
- Is it a layered sound? Can it be made by one person or does it need a group? (Bats and birds are a good example of this as there's the option of flapping wings as well as a squeak or chirp.)
- ... and don't forget, explore 'strange' sounds from your students. There is always one who can make the most interesting—albeit most annoying!—sound. Put it to good use, perhaps even telling a story completely in sound.

▣ Music-reading: how soon is too soon?

Reading music is an aural as well as a physical process and I believe in teaching these skills from the beginning. Initially, I introduce rhythm and melody separately, sometimes using them as a way to introduce a new song or reinforce one already learnt. I like using rhythm syllables and sol-fa (or numbers) as they produce results that last, but I'm not obsessive about it. Unless your school is extremely supportive, your music coordinator is really a music educator, and you allot more than 30 minutes a week to your music lessons, there will be a limit as to how much can be achieved and how quickly—but you can achieve, and I think you should try!

▧ Rhythm

Rhythm syllables

I use two varieties of rhythm syllables. The initial set includes 1-beat/pulse notes, based on insects; the second set is more traditional. There are other variations, but I've found these the most useful.

crotchet	quavers	crotchet rest	semiquavers	quaver/crotchet/ quaver
slug ta	spi-der ti - ti	sh (sleeping slug) sh	ca-ter-pil-lar ti-ka-ti-ka	syn-co - pa

I like the insect version as the symbols look (in a abstract way) like what they represent and younger singers cope well with them. I also like using this version without the notehead, as the rhythm cards can be used upside down as well and I don't have to make two sets.

- OK, *Mother goose* may not be your first choice of literary classic, but rhymes can be very useful for understanding the rhythm of the words and transferring words to recognizable rhythm patterns. These are the first patterns I use and some of the rhymes they come from. (Be aware: I've separated the following into 4-beat/pulse groupings and not necessarily by phrase length.)

Star light, star bright
First star I see tonight
Wish I may, wish I might
Have the wish I wish tonight.

Rain, rain go away
Come again another day.

Fudge, fudge, call the judge
Mama's got a baby.
Not a boy, not a girl
Just a plain old baby.

Mr East gave a feast
Mr North laid the cloth
Mr West did his best
Mr South burnt his mouth
Eating cold potato.

Bounce high, bounce low
Bounce the ball to Shiloh.

Peas porridge hot
Peas porridge cold
Peas porridge in the pot
Nine days old.

- Clap a 4-beat pattern while saying the rhythm syllables; the group echoes.
- Clap a pattern (without saying the syllables); the group responds by saying the syllables.
- What's the song? Clap the rhythm of a song/poem your group knows well and see if they can guess what it is. This gets their brains thinking about the text and the rhythm of the words.
- Make cards of each of the rhythms (don't worry, they needn't be artistic). Use the cards to:

○ Reinforce the rhythm of songs your group already knows. Figure out the rhythm of a song or poem, then—using the correct cards—mix them up and get your group to put them back in the correct order.

○ Use them as ostinato patterns to accompany your repertoire.

○ Use them for developing reading skills. Read each card individually, then join several cards together to make a phrase. Try reading this phrase backwards, or read it in two parts, forwards and backwards at the same time.

Practice patterns

These patterns are more formal and are written with traditional notation on a one-line staff. They can be introduced after your group is familiar with the basic notation, and you can use either type of rhythm syllable to read them. Of course, you and your group can make up your own patterns too; let your current song and poem materials be your guide.

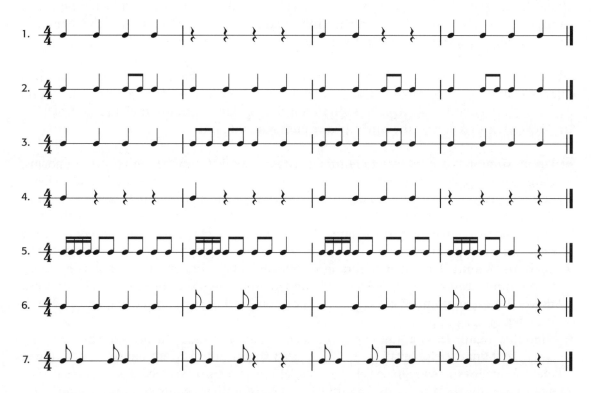

● Numbers 1–4/5 are for any age group if you have prepared by using the previous rhythm exercises. Numbers 5–6/7 can be added at the upper end of this age group, but make sure you've done song/poem material that includes the syn-co-pa patterns (such as No. 12 'Fun mje alafia and Canoe song') before using 6 and 7.

● Read the patterns forwards or backwards.

● Read them forwards and backwards in combination.

● Read them in canon (as a round) and try starting the second part in different places (after 2 bars, after 1 bar, after 2 beats, and so on).

● Pick a rhythm pattern from an electronic keyboard and use it as a backing when reading the patterns.

● Use them as ostinato patterns to accompany songs.

● Sing them as a drone (on one pitch), as this will help to reinforce matching pitch within a group.

The Singing Voice

Matching pitch

Developing singing skills is a question not only of finding the 'singing voice' but also of becoming aware, using, and differentiating between all types of vocal qualities—speaking, yelling, whispering, imitating accents (cowboy, posh, 'famous mouse'), and the like. Once there is a singing quality, then matching pitch becomes another focus of learning to sing. Being able to match pitch and maintain a key while singing is a double skill when singing alone and singing within a group. Some children will find their singing and matching voices easily, while others will struggle. All learning takes time, and although we can help and support our groups, this will take as long as it takes.

I have never really had a student who is 'tone deaf', but I have had students who had difficulty finding their singing voices, and I have had lots more students who found matching pitch a real challenge. This requires listening skills, both internal and external. Try these exercises to reinforce the singing voice and matching pitch:

- **Drone singing** is a good way to reinforce listening skills for matching pitch. Use poems, tongue-twisters, counting, reciting the alphabet, etc., and sing on one pitch, like a chant. Choose a comfortable pitch to begin on and change the starting pitch (gradually up or down) with each repetition. This encourages the whole group to listen and match pitch, while gradually increasing their range. Without a melody, the voice and ears can really concentrate on pitch.
- **Surround sound.** If a singer is finding it difficult to pitch, carefully move strong singers to positions nearby (stereo or even surround sound). You don't need to be obvious, but they will hear and imitate better in these positions, rather than on the end of a row or at the back of the group.
- **'Hello, who am I?'** is a guessing-game song. One child hides their eyes while another sings the phrase 'hello, who am I?'. They get two guesses to figure out who sang. (Trust me, two guesses is enough, or else no one else gets a turn. We also keep score: if they guess correctly, the group gets a point; if not, I do, but they usually end up winning.)
- **Extend 'hello, who am I'** into a call and response. Use the text as a daily greeting to your group, or substitute a specific name—'hello Sarah, who am I?'—and ask for a solo response. Try recording your group singing this together and individually at the beginning of the school year. Leave a couple of seconds between each recording for practice 'guessing' time when they listen to it. It's exciting to hear how we sound when recorded, and we often don't hear ourselves the way others do. For this age group it will probably be a new experience. Towards the end of the school year, listen to the recording again and see if the children recognize one other. This age group grows and develops very quickly; voices change, and I think you will all be surprised.

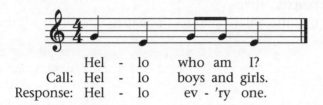

▢ Melody

Staves and hand signs

Looking at and making sense of notes on a stave can appear a daunting process. But it is a process and is very logical. I like the syllables of sol-fa (doh, ray, me, fa, so, la, te) but I prefer to use numbers (1, 2, 3, 4, 5, 6, 7) to teach sight-singing, which I introduce to all my groups. The syllables produce a more natural singing sound as they emphasize vowels more than the numbers do, but the numbers make understanding the distance between sounds (intervals) more obvious. I've used both ways with all age groups, but I always include hand signs as part of the learning process. Hand signs kinaesthetically 'anchor' the brain and body to the sound.

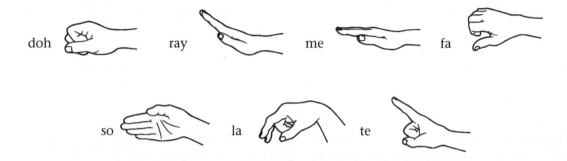

Hand sign drawings reproduced with permission of the British Kodály Academy,
© Copyright British Kodály Academy, London 2000.

Hand signs require a fine motor skill which some younger singers find difficult. With this age group try using both hands symmetrically as this will be a bit easier—my students seem to make the signs more clearly with two hands than with one. This will also prepare them for later years, when they will watch two hands when singing in two parts. It will also prepare them for watching and reacting to a conductor, and it's never too early to prepare for that!

Don't worry, you don't have to introduce all the hand signs to this group. Working with la, so, and me, with options for using ray and doh, can be enough to begin with. The following list shows the order in which the signs are frequently introduced, the age groups to introduce them to, and an example of an appropriate song. This is a guide and not a hard-and-fast rule. Do what you are comfortable with, and as you become more confident extend what you use.

- so, me (5–6 years)   'Star light', from No. 18 'Two night-time songs')
- la, so, me (6–7 years)   No. 4 'The mill-wheel and the snail'
- la, so, me, doh (7 and up)   No. 11 'On a log'
- so, me, doh (7 and up)   No. 16 'I see the moon'
- la, so, me, ray, doh (7 and up) No. 14 'Great big house'

▢ Solo singing, teachers' voices, and working in parts

Our goal is to encourage young singers to feel confident and proud about their voices as they explore and develop them. In working towards this goal, the singers need to feel respect for themselves as well as those singing with them. Grown-ups (and especially teachers) seem to be the first to say 'I can't sing, I'm tone deaf', when of course they do sing and are most likely not tone deaf!

Being supportive about developing young voices also means you have to be supportive to your own voice and willing to really sing with your group, so solo singing begins with you. Enjoy the singing, and be gentle with yourself. This isn't about being a professional singer; this is about tapping into that pleasure most of us feel when we sing when we're alone.

Solo work can be as simple as just asking a child to sing back their name ('The name game' p. xv) or take one phrase of a song (No. 14 'Great big house')—short and simple. This will help the children to develop their confidence and respect for others and their voices. To help build the confidence of those who are reticent, encourage them to sing a short song, or a portion of a song (No. 30 'The ants go marching'). If a student is unwilling to sing alone, they can sing in pairs or small groups; encourage, but don't force.

Working in parts is basically about layering the sounds of voices or instruments together. It's the idea of getting used to hearing more than one sound/timbre at the same time and finding your place within that sound.

Adding a percussion part can be a good way of adding another layer of sound and gets the young performer to understand the concept of how sounds can work together. Try the following:

- Sing while another sound (or two) plays (No. 6 'Bobby Shafto').
- Sing and maintain a steady pulse at the same time (No. 10 'Indian drum').
- Sing and transfer the pulse to a percussion instrument (No. 3 'Naughty pussy-cat').
- Add a rhythmic ostinato shared by several instruments (No. 5 'Squirrel songs').

Layering singing sounds can be a bit more daunting, but it's basically the same concept. Using something that grows out of the tune as an additional part not only reinforces the tune/text but makes it easier to maintain the additional part, as these songs do:

- Layering vocal ostinati (No. 11 'On a log').
- Speaking in a round (No. 14 'Great big house'—'Simple Simon' poem).
- Singing in a round (No. 27 'Hotaru koi').
- Using a repeated sung phrase (No. 16 'I see the moon').
- Partner tune/poem (No. 19 'Rabbits').
- Reinforcing the tune but in a new individual part (No. 18 'Two night-time songs').

When singing a round you'll sometimes see a child cover their ears to block out all sound but their own. Gently discourage this, as the idea is to listen to and 'be part of' the whole sound. This is a skill that takes time and will be more challenging with each layer added.

Some final thoughts

You don't have to do everything at once. Take your time, and don't be limited by the ideas in this book. Develop your own ideas, and explore them with your groups. Review, revisit, and enjoy!

Section 1

Move that Voice

1 Mr Wiggly and Mr Waggly

RESOURCES ▶ CD track 2

☐ Information

This is an easy and enjoyable finger-play for helping students to explore the range of their voices and different pitch directions. I learned this at a Kodály class in the US, and was excited to see how much could be achieved with such a seemingly simple game. I often use this close to the beginning of a session, and with children up to key stage 2 (8–9 years). It's a great piece for developing concentration skills, and the silences in the 'have a listen' sections are just as important as the sounds—maybe more so.

☐ Starting

- Get a feel for the story by listening to the CD.

☐ Teaching and rehearsing

Day 1

- Tell the story for 'Day 1' with all the accompanying movements and sounds, gradually encouraging the group to join in. Start with thumbs up for 'This is Mr Wiggly/Mr Waggly', then open your hand for 'opens the door', tuck your thumb across your palm for 'steps inside', and close your hand for 'shuts the door'. Since this last action requires a finer motor skill, it may take a while for some groups to do this comfortably with both hands.
- Take your time telling the story, especially the slides up and down the hill. Try to make these hills about an octave; begin at a comfortable speaking-voice pitch, and then slide slowly. This will get the vocal folds to gradually speed up and slow down, raising and lowering the pitch. This is a great exercise for widening the vocal range.
- Take care to make a difference between the spoken sections and the rhythmic ones.

Day 2

- The next day, Mr Waggly decides to visit Mr Wiggly. Repeat the story, but this time press the buzzer instead of ringing the doorbell.

Day 3

- Now Mr Wiggly decides to visit Mr Waggly at the same time Mr Waggly decides to visit Mr Wiggly. They meet, but even in this version there are three hills!

- Get those tongues moving with the 'knocking' clicks. Explore how the knocks sound with the tongue in different areas of the mouth. A forward placement with a smiling face will give a higher pitch than the tongue in the roof of the mouth with a long face.
- Don't forget the silences. Wait and listen for an answer after knocking at the door, and make it a real silence. This will help to set up concentration skills for all future work.
- Enjoy the surprise aspect of the bell sound. This introduces one of the first conscious intervals leading to sight-singing development, the falling minor third, and the buzzer can help lead to exploration of all the delightful or gross sounds that can be made with the lips, teeth, and tongue.

☐ Ideas

- When the two characters finally meet, they might have a conversation. As this story makes an excellent warm-up exercise, this might introduce the next activity in your lesson plan. The sillier the better!
- Be adventurous. Maybe the next time you tell the story, they travel a different way, always making the appropriate vocal shape. For example:

through the tunnel   over the bridge

- They might even take a different mode of transport (aeroplane, car, boat, train, walk), using the appropriate sound, or even travel through an imaginary landscape—perhaps they have a day at the beach?—always exploring possible sounds vocally.

- This is a great piece for developing a graphic score of your journey and the sounds along the way. It's never too early to start preparing skills for reading music.

children' splashing ...   shovelling sand ...   snoozing ...   big ship ...   donkey
        sea-gulls calling ...   sailing boat ...   flock of birds ...   lighthouse ...

🔲 Listen out

- Listen to the individuals in your group. Who is able to make the 'hill' shape with their voices, and who is finding it more difficult? Gradually encourage the group to make higher hills and to begin to control the pitch shapes. This will help each child to find their singing voice and to differentiate it from their speaking voice.

🔲 Performing

- This is really more appropriate as a warm up, but if you have developed a graphic score it would be interesting to exchange scores with another group and perform for each other.

1 Mr Wiggly and Mr Waggly

Anon.

This is Mr Wiggly (*R thumb up*), this is Mr Waggly (*L thumb up*).

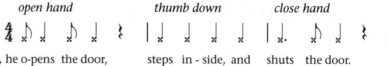

Whenever Mr Wiggly wants to go into his house, he o-pens the door, steps in - side, and shuts the door.

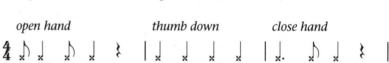

Whenever Mr Waggly wants to go into his house, he o-pens the door, steps in - side, and shuts the door.

Day 1

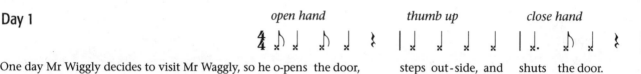

One day Mr Wiggly decides to visit Mr Waggly, so he o-pens the door, steps out-side, and shuts the door.

Then he goes

thumb traces hill 3x

When he gets there, he knocks on the door three times, very politely:

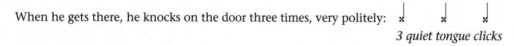

3 quiet tongue clicks

Have a listen ... (*no sound*)

Let's knock a little harder:

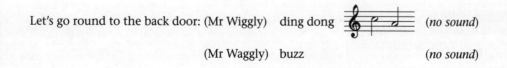

3 louder tongue clicks

Have a listen ... (*no sound*)

Let's go round to the back door: (Mr Wiggly)   ding dong   (*no sound*)

(Mr Waggly)   buzz   (*no sound*)

(*thumb talking!*) 'I guess I'll have to go home'. Then he goes

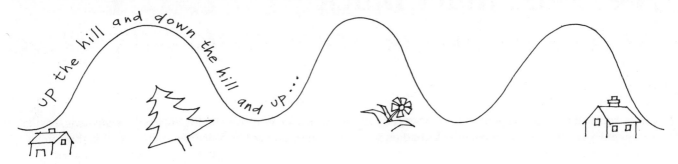

thumb traces hill 3x

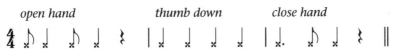

When Mr Wiggly gets home, he o-pens the door,   steps in - side, and   shuts   the door.

Day 2

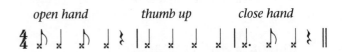

The next day, Mr Waggly (*L thumb*) decides to visit Mr Wiggly, so he o-pens the door,   steps out-side, and shuts the door.

Then he goes

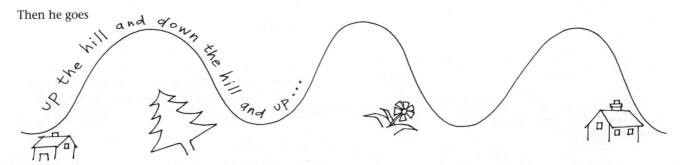

thumb traces hill 3x

(*Continue as for Day 1, except when you go to the back door it's a buzz not a bell.*)

Day 3

The next day, Mr Wiggly decides to visit Mr Waggly
at the same time Mr Waggly decides to visit Mr Wiggly, so they o-pen the door,   step out-side, and   shut the door.

Then they go

L thumb traces hill 3x   *R thumb traces hill 3x*

(*There are still three hills, yet this time Mr Wiggly and Mr Waggly meet in the middle of their journey!*)

This page may be photocopied

2 Miss Mary Mack

RESOURCES ▶ CD track 3

Information

This is a great song with clapping patterns, rhyming words, and lots of repetition, popular with children around the world. It will help your group to practise keeping a steady pulse and to find their matching-pitch voices. The gradually more complex clapping patterns, with and without partners, develop not only motor skills but also left-brain/right-brain coordination.

Starting

• Keep a steady patching pulse while getting the group to echo-sing each line in call-and-response style. This is about internally feeling and maintaining that steady pulse.

Teaching and rehearsing

• You won't need to echo-sing more than once or twice as the group will naturally join in. As you sing each line, keep the diction clear, concentrating on the repeated words and especially the endings of those words.
• Gradually let the group sing it on their own. To get them started, see if they can remember the repeated words.
• The song is made up of a simple four-note pattern, up and down, with repeated notes at the end of each phrase. Because of this limited range and simple pattern, you can vary the starting pitch anywhere from D to G (G major/A major/B flat major/C major) and should reinforce matching pitch within the group.
• Vary the steady patching pulse pattern with the individual clapping patterns suggested. Notice that these are on two levels—patsch/down, clap/up—with the combinations changing. As the group gains confidence, try the partner clapping patterns.

Ideas

• First steps in part-singing are ideal for this song. Divide the group in two, one side singing the first three notes of each phrase and the other responding with the repeated words, then repeat, reversing the group tasks. As your young singers develop they might even do one of these parts as a solo in a non-threatening way. When they sing as individuals or in smaller groups you'll be able to keep aware of who is finding their singing voice and matching-pitch voice, and who is finding this a challenge.
• Develop your own accompanying patterns with your group, gradually working towards the challenging patterns. Try to include the 'shoulder cross' movement, as this crosses the mid-line of the body and really works left-brain/right-brain coordination.
• Encourage your group to practise the patterns with a partner outside of class time.

Listen out

• Some young singers will find it easy to maintain a steady pulse and sing with a matching pitch, while others will find this a challenge. It simply takes as long as it takes. Be patient with your singers, as well as with yourself.

Performing

• This isn't really a piece for performance, but it could be done with the piano accompaniment and with a different clapping pattern in each verse, perhaps with the patterns becoming more complex. If you're feeling a little 'crazy' you could get your audience to accompany the singing, trying each of the patterns!

2 Miss Mary Mack

Trad. American

Clapping patterns

Individual   **Partner**   **Challenging**

Key

Clap	C
Patsch	P
Partner clap	PC
Shoulder cross	SC

This page may be photocopied

3 Naughty pussy-cat

RESOURCES ▶ CD track 4

☐ Information

This singing game is based on the perennial favourite 'Duck, duck, goose'. With a very limited range, mostly just two notes and a final downward pattern, it's easy to sing and very repeatable. Changing the starting pitch with every few repetitions will gradually extend your singers' vocal range, and as the song is very short, there's plenty of chance for them to take their turn in the game.

☐ Teaching and rehearsing

- Sing the song with the actions and then repeat it, encouraging the group to join in. Young singers learn this song very quickly. Take your time with this song and repeat it many times.
- The downward pattern of the last line will come quite easily, but it could be a bit under the pitch and out of tune. If while singing this line you raise your forearms (as if you are lifting something heavy) you will engage the muscles in the mid-region of the body, which will support the song and improve the tuning.
- The other three phrases fluctuate up and down the interval of a 2nd, but most young singers will gradually pitch these correctly, and they will improve if you take care over the diction. Also, enjoy the final 't' of 'cat', 'fat', and 'scat'.
- The piano/guitar accompaniment is optional but can help to reinforce pitch.

☐ Ideas

- Add the game. The group should stand in a circle singing the song, while one child walks around the outside of the circle until the word 'scat!', and then taps the shoulder of the closest person. The game then becomes a chase around the circle until they get back to the empty space. If the 'tapper' gets back first, they're safe and sit down in place. If not, they go to the centre of the circle and sit for the next repeat of the game—still joining in with the singing—then return to the circle and sit down. The 'chaser' then becomes the new person walking around the outside of the circle, and the game begins again. If the children sit after their turn it's easy to see who is yet to have a turn, but they should still sing.

- A nice variation when the song is unaccompanied is to have two xylophones (bass ones would be great, but alto will do better than soprano) in the centre of the circle. The teacher is at one and a student at the other, maintaining a steady pulse for one game, until another student has a turn in the circle. These accompanying ostinati will be very successful if you have the whole group do the actions first.
- This will be a song you'll return to after introducing the rhythm elements │ ⊓ ⼂, singing the song on rhythm syllables (see p. xviii).
- The song can also be sung in a round, with the second voice beginning at *.

☐ Listen out

- As the group becomes more involved in the game, be careful that the 'singing' voice doesn't become the 'shouting' voice.
- Vary the dynamics (volume) in each repetition to encourage nice singing and control.

☐ Performance

- Although this is not a traditional performance piece, it could be used as part of a selection of songs being learned at this level, with or without accompaniment. Any occasion can be a performance. The point is that the singing, wherever it is done, should be joyful and in tune, with clear words and sung with 'heart'.

3 Naughty pussy-cat

Trad. American

Scolding! ♩ = 88

Naugh-ty pus-sy-cat! You are ve-ry fat!

You have but-ter on your whis-kers, Naugh-ty pus-sy-cat. *Scat!*

Ostinati

Actions

Patsch

Clap
Patsch

Xylophone

1.

or 2.

(click mallets)

4 The mill-wheel and the snail

RESOURCES ▶ CD track 5

▢ Information

These two songs both have a circle theme, evoking the circling of a mill-wheel in the picturesque countryside, and children playing near a river's edge, finding snails and their empty shells. The three-note range gives the songs a winding quality and a real feel of circles, and the optional group movements are a great way of internalizing a steady pulse.

▢ Starting

- Play or sing the tune to your group as they walk around the room in time to the pulse.

▢ Teaching and rehearsing

- Start with 'Mill-wheel', unaccompanied, singing in a clear and steady voice and taking a breath on the rest at the end of each two-bar phrase.
- With their three-note range and simple rhythms which follow the rhythm of the words, these songs provide an opportunity to develop aural awareness. As you sing each song, add the modified hand signs shown below (a quiet click, clap, and patsch) to reinforce the vocal shape. Make the hand signs as quietly as possible. They should not be a body-percussion accompaniment, just an outline of the vocal shape. Take the time to do this with both songs.

- Sing both songs unaccompanied, starting on A, and then move the starting pitch to G, F, and E (C major, B flat major, and A major). Then add the piano to reinforce the melody in 'Mill-wheel' but drop out for 'Snail'. This gives your singers an opportunity to maintain the pitch on their own. By alternating between the two songs, their pitch-sense will grow stronger.

▢ Ideas

- Join hands in a long line and all sing while everyone follows you. Still holding hands (and yes, this will be a challenge!), weave around your space, but not too quickly, gradually finishing in a standing circle. This will probably take several repetitions of the song. Change leaders, making sure that whoever leads keeps the group 'safe'. Try this with smaller groups, even partners, and reinforce the safety aspect.
- When your group can manage the space well, extend the movement to include 'winding up' like a snail shell, and then unwinding.

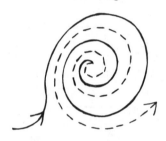

- When your group can sing both songs confidently, try hand signing while inner-hearing the words and melody. This is a good way to develop inner listening skills.
- When your young singers are familiar with the singing pattern so, la, me, consider using this song as one of the first pieces for developing sight-singing and copy the three-line stave shown above on the board or on a poster (writing the repeats in full). This is a great extender for later key stage 1 and early key stage 2.

▢ Listen out

- Again, this is a song for matching pitch within the group. It also promotes group cooperation and space management.
- Be aware where the 'breaths' are taken and make sure they are calm, silent breaths.

▢ Performing

- Perform the piece one song after the other, at an even tempo. You'll know it's too fast if the quavers/eighth notes are uncomfortable to sing, or too slow if the group runs out of breath too easily. Gradually move through each of the keys, maintaining a steady pulse and pitch, then sing the songs with hand signs using either words or sol-fa syllables.

4 The mill-wheel and the snail

Mill-wheel

Trad. American

Flowing ♩ = 80

Round and round the wheel goes round, as it turns the corn is ground.

Snail

Snail, snail, snail, snail, creep - ing round and round and round,

3

snail, snail, snail, snail, creep - ing round and round and round.

Try singing in these keys:

C major   Bb major   A major

5 Squirrel songs

RESOURCES ▶ CD track 6

Information

These two contrasting squirrel songs work well alone or, when sung together, offer a satisfying and accessible way into part-singing. The accompanying percussion ostinato has the feel of a quiet, still squirrel, and then a squirrel quickly running up a tree. These are good songs for reinforcing melody shapes and basic sight-singing skills.

Starting

- Start by learning the drum, shaker, and guiro ostinato patterns. Teach them as a body-percussion pattern first (drum = patsch, shaker = clap, guiro = click):

- ○ Start with just the patching ﹨ Z ﹨ Z , saying the rhythm syllables (slug, *sh*, slug, *sh*, or ta, *sh*, ta, *sh*).
- ○ Then transfer some children to the drum, eventually inner-hearing the syllables.
- ○ Do the same process with the other two instruments, shaker (*clap*) and guiro (*click*).

Let us chase the squirrel

- Hand sign and sing 1, 2, 1 (doh, ray, doh), then sing 'up the hickory tree' while hand signing.
- Sing the song to your group, asking them to listen carefully and see if they can join in when they hear 'up the hickory tree'. Try this a couple of times, then sing the whole song together.

Hop old squirrel

- Hand sign and sing 3, 3, 3 (me, me, me), then sing 'hop old squirrel' while hand signing.
- Sing the song to the group, and invite them (with an open hand) to join in with this line; do this several times, gradually adding the 'eidledum's.

Teaching and rehearsing

- When the songs can be sung confidently, add the percussion parts. Wait until the group can sing the song while doing each pattern before adding the next one. This will probably need to be done over several sessions.

Listen out

- Make sure the group is making a really nice singing sound throughout the songs.
- Try to breathe after each two-bar phrase; this should give enough breath to keep each phrase smooth.
- Watch out for the two-note slur on 'squirrel'; keep it smooth and connected, without punching the last note of the phrase.

Performing

- My arrangement of these songs is a suggestion and not definitive, so feel free to adapt it to the needs of your group. There are lots of elements to work with. Try exploring dynamics (how loudly or quietly they sing) and tempo (how fast or slow they sing). Put the various parts of the arrangement in any order, letting your group decide which to include for each performance.
- Use the instruments you have to hand and experiment with the timbre. What does a scurrying squirrel sound like?

5 Squirrel songs

Let us chase the squirrel

Trad. American
arr. Jo McNally

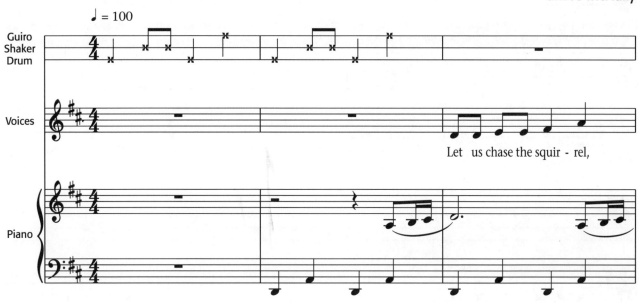

Let us chase the squir - rel,

up the hick-ory, down the hick-ory, let us chase the squir - rel, up the hick-ory tree.

continues overleaf

Hop old squirrel

Hop old squir-rel, ei-dle-dum, ei-dle-dum,

hop old squir-rel, ei-dle-dum dee, hop old squir-rel, ei-dle-dum, ei-dle-dum, hop old squir-rel, ei-dle-dum dee.

Both songs together

Part 1

Hop old squir-rel, ei-dle-dum, ei-dle-dum,

Part 2

Let us chase the squir - rel,

This page may be photocopied

hop old squir-rel, ei-dle-dum dee, hop old squir-rel, ei-dle-dum, ei-dle-dum, hop old squir-rel, ei-dle-dum dee,

up the hick-ory, down the hick-ory, let us chase the squir - rel, up the hick-ory tree,

hop old squir-rel, ei-dle-dum, ei-dle-dum.

up the hick-ory tree.

This page may be photocopied

6 Bobby Shafto

RESOURCES ▶ CD track 7

☐ Information

'Bobby Shafto' is a popular traditional folk-song with a light and lilting tune. It is great fun to sing and is about a 'real' person, Bobby (Robert) Shafto, who lived in County Durham in the eighteenth century. The song has a strong steady pulse and its simple melody uses a sequence over the first three phrases: the first and third phrases have the same melody, while the second phrase shifts the tune down a fourth. This song is an excellent way to develop good group intonation within the range of an octave.

☐ Starting

• Clearly speak the poem in rhythm and then have the group echo-speak the poem by phrase, keeping the rhythm steady. With each repeat of the spoken text—and still echo-speaking—change the quality of the sound, but always keep the text clear. Varying the quality of the sound exercises the vocal folds (thin/thick) and changes the position of the larynx (high/low):
  ◦ whisper the text
  ◦ use your lowest 'monster' voice
  ◦ use a very nasal quality
  ◦ use a 'Mickey Mouse' voice

☐ Teaching and rehearsing

• Reinforce good posture before beginning to sing. Asking the group to 'stand tall and proud' usually evokes a good starting position.
• The tune is easy to learn, so first sing it through unaccompanied. Echo-sing line by line, taking care over the two-note slur on the last word of each of the first three phrases.
• Learn the xylophone part by singing the note names as text. Then alternate singing the song with singing the note names until both parts are well learnt.

• Divide the group in two, with one group on the tune and the other on the instrumental part. Before trying both parts together, start the xylophone with the piano accompaniment then add the vocal line on the repeat.

☐ Ideas

• Explore dynamics with this song. Think about travelling on a ship. The closer the ship the louder the sound, the further away the quieter the sound. How loudly or quietly can you sing the song without yelling or whispering? It takes control and a supported sound to vary the dynamic but maintain a clear singing voice.

☐ Listen out

• Although the tune is very accessible, it can be difficult to sing nicely with good intonation and musical phrases. The melody is made up of mostly quavers/eighth notes, with lots of interval leaps in each line. This can sometimes make the singing feel choppy and disjointed. If this happens, try adding a smooth, circular arm movement for each phrase.

☐ Performing

Put it all together!
• As an opening section, start by speaking the poem using the different vocal qualities (whispering, using a 'monster' voice, and so on).
• Then sing the song twice, with a different dynamic each time.
• Play the xylophone part, and have the group sing along with the note names.
• Finally, sing the song accompanied by the xylophone.

6 Bobby Shafto

Trad. English

(clap, clap, clap, clap) Bob-by Shaf-to's gone to sea,— Sil-ver buck-les on his knee,

He'll come back and mar-ry me,— Bon-ny Bob-by Shaf - to.

Xylophone

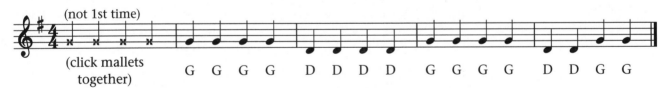

(not 1st time)

(click mallets together)   G G G G   D D D D   G G G G   D D G G

7 Old King Glory

Information

This song reinforces steady pulse and has a very cheerful melody incorporating octave leaps to gently stretch that vocal range. It is a song most groups will never tire of singing, especially when the movement is added.

Starting

- Start with a little stretching! Gently stretch your arms high and wiggle your fingers, then gently stretch low, bending your knees and touching your toes. Do this several times.

Teaching and rehearsing

- Standing in a circle, count to eight, then march in place for eight beats until the word 'first'.
- Sing the whole song for the group, gradually encouraging them to join in.
- Sing the song and march until the word 'first', then stretch high on the words 'first' and 'second'.
- This time sing the song as above, but add a clap on the word 'third'.

- Take your time putting together the song and the actions. Remember, everything may not work the first time. Sometimes it takes care and repetition—even many repetitions.

Ideas

- Change the word 'Glory' to your name, changing 'King' to 'Queen' if necessary.
- This is a nice twist on a circle game. The group remains stationary while one person goes around the outside tapping the closest person in the circle as they get to 'the first one', 'the second one', and 'the third come with me'. The third person now becomes the leader, taking the hand of the previous leader, so at each repetition the line becomes longer but builds on from the front.

Listen out

- It's going to be the tuning of the octaves, but don't panic. This song is for starting to stretch to the octave, so it will take a few sessions to get the singers in tune.

7 Old King Glory

Trad. American

Confidently ♩ = 112

Old King Glo - ry of the moun - tain, the moun - tain was so high it near - ly touched the sky, the first one the se - cond one the third come with me.

This page may be photocopied

8 Chicken on a fencepost

RESOURCES ▶ CD track 9

Information

This is a great rhythmic song with words that are 'delicious' to say and sing. It really gets the lips, teeth, and tongue coordinated. With the first three lines of text repeated and a very simple melody, it's fun to sing and move to.

Starting

• Introduce the piece using spoken rhythm syllables.

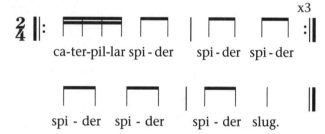

ca-ter-pil-lar spi - der   spi - der spi - der

spi - der   spi - der   spi - der slug.

• Adding the actions suggested below, keep a steady pulse while you echo-speak each bar using very clear diction and vibrant voice.

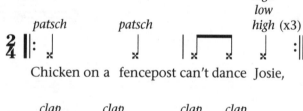

Chicken on a   fencepost can't dance Josie,

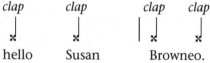

hello   Susan   Browneo.

Teaching and rehearsing

• Speak each two-bar phrase in rhythm at least three times, varying the dynamics (loud/soft/whisper) and keeping the pulse even and not too fast (Andante, or at a walking pace).
• Gradually work until the group can comfortably say the whole text. The repetition of the first line will feel like a tongue-twister, so take your time and don't forget to enjoy!
• Teach and rehearse the song unaccompanied.
• Sing the song while doing the body-percussion pattern suggested above. Maintaining the pattern will reinforce the pitch direction at the end of each line (up/down/up).

Ideas

• Singing unaccompanied, vary the starting pitch.
• Do as a two-part piece. One group sings 'Chicken on a fencepost' and the other group answers 'can't dance Josie'. Vary the size of the groups doing each part, and encourage someone to sing one of the parts as a solo.
• Sing in canon, with the second part starting at *. Take the canon part yourself first so the group can hear what the two parts sound like together, then invite a few singers to join you. Switch parts (your group starts first).
• Sing the song with the accompanying movements. Eventually you'll want to try this in a circle, but try it first with everyone facing you and moving in the same direction. This will be fun and challenging!
  ○ Step to the side (moving one leg only) with your hands apart, then clap as you move the other leg to bring your feet together. Repeat this three times moving in one direction, then finish with four claps on the words 'hello Susan Browneo'.
  ○ Repeat the song, moving in the other direction.
  ○ Try the movement in a circle.
  ○ Try the movement with partners facing each other.

Listen out

• Diction! Keep it crisp and clean. Practising with the rhythm syllables keeps the tongue forward in the mouth and works the tip of the tongue.

Performing

There are many elements in this song. Here's one suggestion for how they might be put together:
• Sing the song.
• Sing two verses while doing the movement.
• Sing a verse in canon (with or without the movement).
• Sing a verse using the rhythm syllables (slug, caterpillar, spider), without the movement.
• Repeat the final phrase of the rhythm syllables—spider spider spider slug—gradually getting quieter until you finish in silence.

8 Chicken on a fencepost

Trad. American

Key

open step to the side, with hands and feet apart
close move the other leg to put feet together, and clap

This page may be photocopied

Section 2

Keep the Beat

9 Warm up and Stomp canon

RESOURCES ▶ CD track 10

▢ Information

I wanted a way to begin warming up the voice and body without resorting to 'traditional' warm ups that may not be so suitable for young singers. So, I came up with this, in two parts—a stretching warm up with varying vocal qualities, and a very simple movement canon. When done together, they not only reinforce group listening skills but also maintain a strong steady pulse. This is an enjoyable, useful piece that can be used effectively with almost all age groups.

▢ Starting

• Before you start to teach this piece, listen to the CD to get a feel for the fun voices.

▢ Teaching and rehearsing

Warm up

• Teach this by rote, using the different vocal qualities (cowboy, posh, whisper, nasal) and doing the actions. Remember, changing the vocal qualities exercises the vocal folds.

Stomp Canon

• The easiest way to teach this is to gradually add each new activity so the piece becomes longer and longer:
  1. Count to eight in a steady pulse.
  2. Count to eight, then march/stomp for eight.
  3. Count to eight, march/stomp for eight, patsch for eight.
  4. Count to eight, march/stomp for eight, patsch for eight, clap for eight.
  5. Count to eight, march/stomp for eight, patsch for eight, clap for eight, click for eight.
  6. All the above and then a turn. There should be one turn taking eight counts to complete.
  7. All the above, then seven 'oo' (monkey) sounds and one loud 'yeah!' The 'oo' sounds should be loud and accompanied by jumping. This will need to be practised several times, and on the final 'yeah!' everyone should freeze with hands high.

• Once the piece is learnt, try doing it as a round. The second group begins after the first has finished counting.

▢ Ideas

• The piano part is meant only to keep the pulse, so feel free to adapt it as you like; anything that keeps a steady beat will be fine.
• Try doing a 'bouncy' (bend knees) not just for the marching but while patsching, clapping, and clicking too. This will help to keep the pulse steady.
• Do just the movements (no vocals) to your favourite CD!
• The 'Warm up' can also be sung in a round, beginning after four bars. For older singers, try starting after two bars!

▢ Listen out

• Take care over the nasal 'ee' sounds, and try to access a 'head voice' rather than produce a pinched and constricted sound. Keep the pitch within the spoken range—think wicked witch sounds!
• When stomping, the tendency will be for some of your group to jump or stomp so hard that they cannot keep a steady pulse. If this happens, or if you think it might happen, call it marching; this should keep things under control.
• The turn can be a bit silly, so you might want to try this with the group before adding the other elements. There will always be at least one child who will try to turn eight times!

▢ Performing

• The first time this piece was performed it was done over two evenings by almost 1,000 singers. We used it as the opening piece for a concert, done first in unison and then in four parts. Not only was it a great way to settle in the singers and warm them up, but, as it's visually fun, it relaxed the audience and prepared everyone for the evening. Sometimes I even repeat it as a closing piece and get the audience to join in!

  Again, this is a piece to consider using for your entire school as a good way to start an assembly and get those voices working before moving on to other group songs. Also, by starting with this your group will get rid of some of the fidgets and nervous energy all age groups can have.

9 Warm up and Stomp canon

Words and music by
Jo McNally

Warm up

This page may be photocopied

Make 'evil' fingers!

13

mf (Nasal voice)

ee ee ee ee   ee ee ee ee   ee ee ee ee   ee ee ee ee

mf

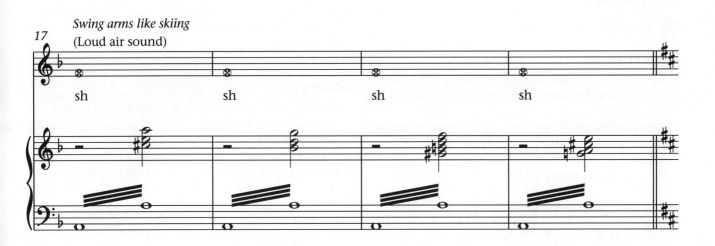

Swing arms like skiing

17

(Loud air sound)

sh   sh   sh   sh

Stomp canon

21

f

| | 1.–6. | | last time | *Hands held high* |

1. *Count 1   2   3   4   5   6   7   8   *oo   oo   oo   Yeah!*
2. Stomp x8
3. Patsch x8
4. Clap x8
5. Click x8
6. Turn (over 8 counts)
7. Jump and say 'oo' x7

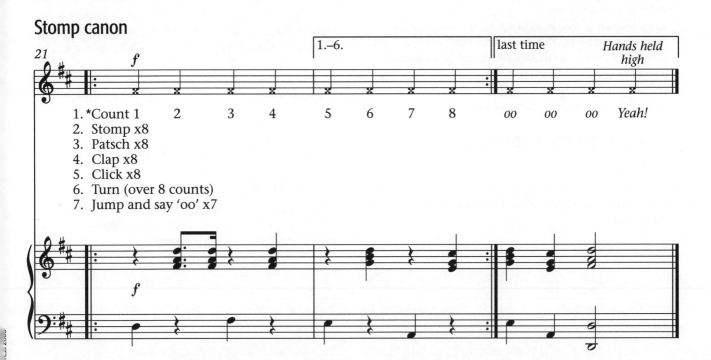

f

* Start canon after the first group has finished counting.

10 Indian drum and Grinding corn

RESOURCES ▶ CD tracks 11 (Indian drum) and 12 (Grinding corn)

▣ Information

Although these songs are not truly Native American, they have the flavour of the style without being disrespectful to the tradition. They provide a good way of not only reinforcing good posture but developing listening and cooperation skills. Both songs are rhythmically strong and emphasize a steady pulse. 'Indian drum' is sung with an outer strength, while 'Grinding corn' is quieter, with an inner strength.

▣ Starting

Indian drum

- Stand 'tall and proud' with hands crossed at the chest (watch those shoulders don't rise but don't make an issue of it).
- Introduce the 'Hi Ho' pattern next; make sure the arms swivel open and down from the elbow, which stays steady.
- Sing the 'Hi Ho' text with the pattern and practise it several times; then add the rest of the song, counting to four twice at the end of the song.

Grinding corn

- Reinforcing the stance of 'tall and proud', start with a grinding pattern. Hands should be closed in a fist and held about chest height.
- Keep a steady pulse, alternating fist on fist in a gentle pounding motion (as in 'one potato two potato ...', but describing circles out to each side in a figure-of-eight). An easier version is to alternate patting each knee, but keep it gentle and quiet.
- Echo-sing the song in two-bar phrases.

▣ Teaching and rehearsing

Indian drum

- Try to sing in four-bar phrases with a strong, confident voice (but not shouted). This will be a little challenging, but keep at it!

- Instead of counting in the last four bars, the leader claps a four-beat pattern while saying the rhythm syllables using only | and ⊓ (slug/ta and spider/ti-ti); the group should then echo this while repeating the rhythm syllables. Try repeating this section as on the CD—four times works well.
- Transfer this pattern to hand-held or free-standing drums. (Be careful with the free-standing drum if you're using mallets, as this could take some coordination.)
- If you have a bass xylophone, the riff will maintain the pulse but be quiet enough to be heard and keep the pitch going.
- Put it all together.

Grinding corn

- Sing the song in two-bar phrases, keeping the singing smooth and gentle.
- Add the pounding gesture on the bass or alto xylophone. For a really lovely timbre, use boomwhackers with the caps (which give the lower octave); this will be a nice contrast with the Indian drum song.
- Put it all together.

▣ Ideas

- If you're feeling very brave, when working on the | and ⊓ patterns in 'Indian drum' give each student a rhythm instrument to echo with: rhythm sticks, tambourines; anything really. This is fun, and very noisy!

▣ Listen out

- Really try to keep the quality of the sound (timbre) different for each piece—strong but not yelled for 'Indian drum', and quite gentle for 'Grinding corn'.

▣ Performing

- These songs work really well as performance pieces, perhaps as part of an Autumn Harvest celebration, alternating between the two songs.

10 Indian drum and Grinding corn

Indian drum

Trad. American

Confidently ♩ = 80
(Xylophone intro.)

hands crossed at chest

This is how the big tall In-dian plays up-on his drum.

L arm R arm open open

Hi Hi

L arm R arm down down — *L arm R arm open open* — *both arms down*

last time: **Fine**

Ho Ho Hi Hi Ho

(Leader/Question)   (Echo/Answer)

(1 2 3 4 1 2 3 4)

Grinding corn

Trad. American

Gently ♩ = 80
(Xylophone intro.)

Rotate fists in a pounding motion

Grind-ing corn, grind-ing corn, Grind-ing corn, grind-ing corn,

1. God of rain and sun and sky, Send the gen-tle but-ter-fly.
2. White and yel-low grain we take, From our har-vest corn-flour make.

Xylophone riff: Indian drum

Alto xylophone

Bass xylophone

Bass xylophone riff: Grinding corn

Indian drum: key

Hands crossed at chest   L/R arm open   L/R arm down

11 On a log

RESOURCES ▶ CD track 13

☐ Information

Singing should be fun, and this very silly rhyming word song is lots of fun to work with. It provides a good opportunity to review rhythm-reading skills, and its 'noisy' ostinato offers an especially good way of internalizing rests.

☐ Teaching and rehearsing

- This is a silly song, so just sing it for your group and let them laugh.
- When you sing it again, ask them to echo the 'noise' rhythms, making sure that you use a voiced 'sh' for each rest.
- On the next repetition, pause just before each animal name and let your group guess it. As the names rhyme with the places, this should be pretty easy. The idea is that with every repetition they remember more of the song and will join in with more each time.
- Using your rhythm cards, echo-clap four-beat patterns using rhythm syllables. Be sure to include rests in the patterns. Here are a few to include:

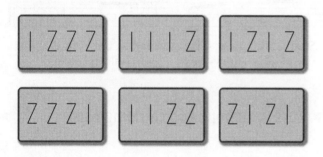

- Hand sign the melody as you sing on numbers or sol-fa (so/la/me or 5/6/3).

☐ Ideas

- Have rhythm cards for each of the 'noise' patterns handy, and as you review each pattern see if your group can match the card to the rhythm.
- Try two rhythms one after the other in a two-bar phrase. Gradually make the phrase longer to include all the rhythm patterns for this song.

☐ Listen out

- Be very careful with the sounds for the bee and the hen as these contain rests. The concept of a rest must be very carefully taught. It has a specific length of time and can often be rushed because it appears there's nothing there. That's why it's good to use the 'sh' at first. Once this has been established, the 'sh' can be transferred to inner hearing.

☐ Performing

- This song works best when done simply. Guitar works well, but use anything that will provide a steady pulse.
- Divide your singers into five groups, one for each character.
- Each group does their 'noise' pattern twice in succession (frog, snake, bee, hen, flea) as an introduction.
- Then everyone sings the song with assigned groups soli on their pattern.
- To finish, layer the patterns. Sing the frog twice, then add the snake twice, and so on, gradually getting louder until you give them a signal to finish.
- If you're very brave, you can allow the sound to deteriorate into utter 'animal sound' chaos! You choose.

11 On a log

Trad. American

noise patterns (x2)

Steady ♩ = 65

1. On a log, lit‑tle frog sang his song the whole night long.

glub glub glub glub

2. On a lake, sneak‑y snake hissed his song as his cake baked.

ss ss ss ss ss

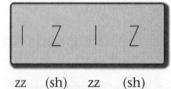

3. By the sea, ti‑ny bee sat and sipped his cup of tea.

zz (sh) zz (sh)

4. In the glen, a big fat hen laid a do‑zen eggs a‑gain.

(sh) cl cl (sh) cl cl

5. On my knee, bit‑sy flea made me itch 'til half past three.

ch ch ch ch ch ch ow!

Bass xylophone

Boomwhacker

12 Fun mje alafia and Canoe song

RESOURCES ▶ CD tracks 14 (Fun mje alafia) and 15 (Canoe song)

◻ Information

These two rhythmically identical songs from different traditions introduce the useful 'syncopa' (♪ | ♪) pattern. 'Fun mje alafia' is a song from Nigeria in the Yoruba language. Loosely translated, it means 'give me happiness, amen, amen'. It is a wonderful two-phrase song, where only the direction of the last note of each phrase is different. Then there's the ever popular 'Canoe song' in a minor key. This song has been used for years for this age group and beyond and is often sung really badly, but it is so useful in your repertoire. Don't try to sing the two songs together; they're not partner tunes!

◻ Teaching and rehearsing

Fun mje alafia

- Start by listening to the CD.
- Sing the song to your group, and then sing it together. Patsch on each 'ashe' (*a - shur*) in bar 2, and circle the hands, like window washing, for the 'ashe' in bar 4. Repeat this several times.
- Now move the body gently side to side each time you sing the words 'fun mje alafia'.
- Put it all together.

Canoe song

- Speak the words in rhythm using especially clear diction. 'Follow the wild goose flight' is a mouthful, so break it down. Try this:

> follow the wild
> follow the wild goose
> follow the wild goose flight
> wild goose, wild goose, wild goose flight

- Echo-sing the song and make sure the word 'silver' is smooth, with the last syllable very quiet. You'll need to do this a few times, echoing each line very carefully. Remember, you're working on listening skills as well as just the text.

◻ Ideas

- Sing the songs with the accompanying ostinato. Have half the group sing the ostinato while the other half sings the tune. Start the pattern before adding the tune.

- Make sure the ostinato group is listening to the tune while they sing, as both parts should finish together. Switch parts.
- Try the ostinato with eyes closed and get those ears working.
- Both songs work well in a canon, starting at *.
- Try the accompanying patterns while singing the songs, but only when each song is very confident. Try singing the song with one pattern per two bars.
- Make up your own four-beat patterns. No need to over-achieve; just four movements is fine! Try the patterns twice as fast, with one pattern per bar.

◻ Listen out

Fun mje alafia

- There are several versions of the words in this song. The version in Yoruba given here was suggested by a Nigerian composer, but I have also heard the song sung with the words 'Fu nke', 'Fu nge', and 'Fu me', and 'oshe' and 'eshe'. There are many different languages in Nigeria and in various areas of a country the dialect timbre can vary. My advice is to go with the given version and to adapt it as appropriate. Of course, you should try to be as accurate as possible when singing multiculturally, but not so particular as to exclude such wonderful songs.

Canoe song

- The problem here is the second phrase, 'flashing with silver', which swoops up the interval of a fourth. This is often sung punchy and loud, destroying the fluid feel to the phrase. Almost every group I've taught the 'Canoe song' to has added a 'paddle the boat' motion without me introducing it; go with the flow.

◻ Performing

- The 'Canoe song' works well as a set with 'Indian drum' and 'Grinding corn', while 'Fun mje alafia' is great for a whole-school assembly warm-up sing!

12 Fun mje alafia and Canoe song

Fun mje alafia

Trad. Yoruba

Fun mje a - la - fi - a   a-she, a - she,__   fun mje a - la - fi - a   a-she, a-she.

Canoe song

Trad. American

My pad - dle's keen and bright,   flash - ing   with   sil - ver.

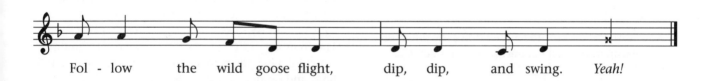

Fol - low   the   wild goose flight,   dip,   dip,   and swing.   *Yeah!*

Ostinati

Fun mje alafia

Fun mje   a - la - fi - a

Canoe song

dip, dip,   and swing. *Yeah!*

Actions

Patsch

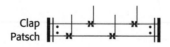

Clap
Patsch

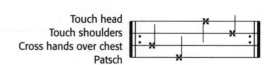

Touch head
Touch shoulders
Cross hands over chest
Patsch

13 I got a letter this morning

RESOURCES ▶ CD track 16

▢ Information

How long can you make a song? Well, with a syncopated rhythm, a catchy tune, and some 'fill in the blanks', you can make it last just about forever—or at least until the session is over! The bonus with this song is that it encourages group matching pitch and gradually singing solo phrases.

▢ Starting

- With the group in a circle, have each student say their name.
- Have the whole group chant the names around the circle on one pitch, with three finger clicks after each name.

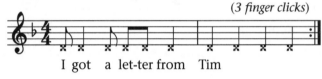

(3 finger clicks)

I got a let-ter from Tim

- Now learn the chorus. To help reinforce the pitch, use thumbs up in the first ending and thumbs down in the second ending.

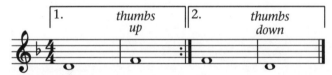

▢ Teaching and rehearsing

- Sing verse 1 for the group, and then sing the chorus together.
- Sing verse 1 again, encouraging the group to join you, and then return to the chorus.
- Do the same for verse 2, remembering to keep using the thumbs up and down for the end of the chorus.

▢ Ideas

- Make cards (letters) of each of your students' first names, and practise reading/chanting the names. Choose four cards to be read for the bridge. Alternate the bridge and the chorus.
- Play 'name tag'. One person says 'I got a letter from _____', filling in the blank, then the named person takes the next 'I got a letter from _____'. Don't forget to put the three finger clicks in after each name. This will allow just enough time for the next person to decide whose name to sing.
- Make up a verse 3!
- This song works well with guitar accompaniment. As it requires only one minor chord (Dm), you can change the key by changing the chord. Try it in Em/Am/Cm.

▢ Listen out

- Ideally sing the chorus in a four-bar phrase. Some of your younger singers will find this difficult, so work towards it. Don't make an issue of it if they need to take a breath, but try to keep it a 'quiet breath', like a secret!
- The chanting of the verse will really help with group matching pitch. Remember, matching takes as long as it takes and cannot be rushed. Be patient.

▢ Performing

- Try it this way, as in the arrangement given here:
  - ~ chorus   ~ chorus
  - ~ verse 1   ~ bridge
  - ~ chorus   ~ chorus
  - ~ verse 2

13 I got a letter this morning

Anon. melody
arr. Jo McNally

With anticipation! ♩ = 118

Chorus

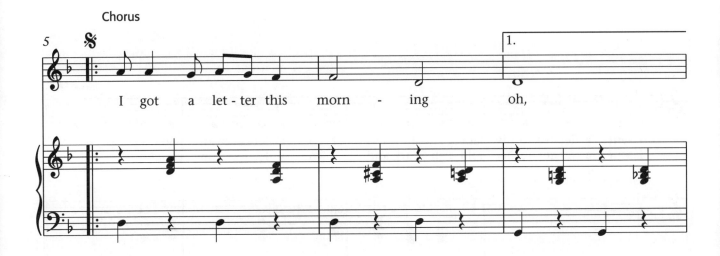

I got a let-ter this morn - ing oh,

After v.2: to Bridge
*last time: **Fine***

yes, oh, yes.

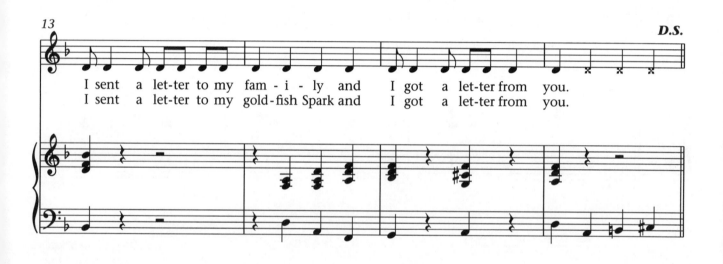

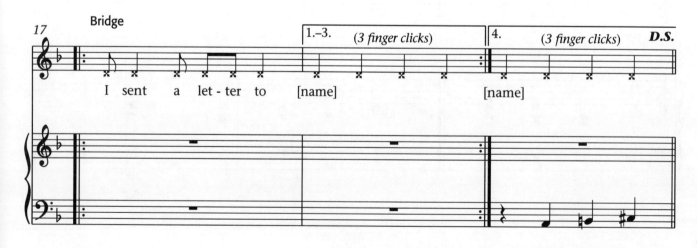

This page may be photocopied

The Singing Voice

14 Great big house

RESOURCES   ▶ CD track 17

☐ Information

This is a fun and rhythmically active song which encourages solo singing with confidence. The tune is catchy, with a repetitive melodic pattern. When combined with the 'Simple Simon' rhyme and the pie ostinato it's a charming yet useful piece.

☐ Starting

- Think of types of pies. Start with pies of the traditional sort, such as fruit pies, and see how many your group can name. Don't be surprised if they suggest some unusual ingredients. My group's suggestions varied from mud pies to nose-with-toes pies, favourite football teams, and some other 'icky' non-food items best left to the imagination!
- Next learn the poem 'Simple Simon'. At the end of the poem ask two to four students to say the name of their favourite pie with the rest of the group echoing the pie name. The echoing keeps everyone involved and 'on task' and this can be done freely without worrying about keeping a steady pulse. If a student is unwilling to participate at this point, just move on to the next one.
- Repeat the poem until everyone has had a turn with a type of pie. It doesn't matter if students choose the same pie. You are trying to encourage working in an ensemble, taking turns, and extending concentration time.
- Introduce the song by echo-singing unaccompanied. With each repetition, change the type of pie.

☐ Teaching and rehearsing

- The goal with each repetition is for a different student to sing the final phrase 'filled with _____ pie' by themselves. This can be as simple as just filling in the type of pie, or singing the entire phrase.
- The trick is to keep the flow of singing without having to stop between verses to choose a new solo singer. So, while singing the first part of the song point to a student and give them the 'thumbs up' sign. If they are willing to sing the final line they will give you the 'thumbs up' sign back and sing. If not, they will give you the 'thumbs down', and you can find another willing singer.
- Continually vary the starting pitch to whatever is comfortable for you, then after several repetitions change the starting pitch up or down. This is best done when the song is unaccompanied.

☐ Listen out

- Don't put pressure on yourself or your group. They will become more comfortable singing by themselves in their own time. It's a matter of gentle encouragement and persistence.
- Don't be too picky about matching pitch the first few times you sing this song. I find that often the group will match quite well, and then the pitch will waver when individuals sing. If you are finding this is a problem, try an energetic 'washing windows' (contrary hand circles) movement on the final phrase, as this will help support the tone. Also, check posture!

☐ Ideas

- Change the town name to your own: 'Great big house in Hil - ling - don/Pa - ris, France/near Swake - leys School'.
- Create your own pie ostinato.
- Try some first steps in simple two-part work.
  - Divide your group in two, and do the song and the 'Simple Simon' rhyme together.
  - Try 'Simple Simon' in canon, starting at *.
  - Try the pie ostinato (repeated) with the poem.

☐ Performing

Combine the various elements:
- Start with the pie ostinato twice.
- Now read the poem expressively, with clear diction.
- Next sing the song, with or without solos; four verses work well.
- Repeat the pie ostinato twice.
- End with the poem, repeating the final phrase 'let me taste your wares' several times, gradually getting quieter until the final phrase is whispered, then stop.

14 Great big house

Trad. American

With gusto! ♩ = 110

Great big house in New Or-leans for-ty stor-ies high____

Ev-'ry room that I've been in filled with pump-kin pie. (clap)

Poem

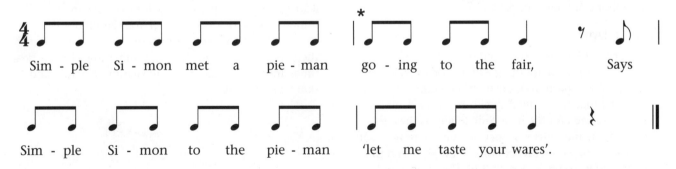

Sim-ple Si-mon met a pie-man go-ing to the fair, Says

Sim-ple Si-mon to the pie-man 'let me taste your wares'.

Pie ostinato

Fudge pie, ap-ple pie, cher-ry pie, yum!

This page may be photocopied

15 Cupboard key

RESOURCES ▶ CD track 18

☐ Information

Learning through exploring and evaluating what you hear and feel as you sing is a process that lasts a lifetime. This deceptively simple two-note singing game in four bars explores control of dynamics and how they affect the quality of the sound; or, when is singing not singing?

☐ Teaching and rehearsing

• This piece is best taught by rote, working with the words first and totally unaccompanied. Whisper, yell, say, and finally sing the text.

• Make sure the pitch for 'somewhere in the classroom' and 'help me find it now' is very clear. Again, sol-fa hand signs, or a similar movement, might be useful here to indicate the high and low pitch.

• Vary the dynamic. Whispering and yelling are naturally quiet/loud. When your group sings the song there will be a natural volume. You can show this by using your hands, palms facing each other but slightly apart. Vary the distance between your hands to show louder (further away) or quieter (closer together).

• Sing the song for your group varying the dynamic, and ask them if it was loud or quiet. Try this several times.

• Now explore with your group how loudly or quietly they can sing before the sound changes from singing to yelling or whispering.

☐ Ideas

• This song works well with a simple guitar accompaniment; also, try keeping the pulse with xylophone or boomwhackers.

Game 1: Dynamics

• Send one child out of the room while you hide an item (I use my keys, but anything will do; for a very young group, have a portion of the item showing). Then sing the song together while the child comes back into the room to search for the item. Sing louder as they get closer to it, and quieter as they get further away. It will probably take several repetitions before they find the item, and it would be wise to limit the number of times you sing the song (four is usually enough). A variation on this is to speak the song in rhythm, again varying the dynamic.

Game 2: Listening skills

• Stand or sit in a circle while one child is in the middle hiding their eyes, and sing the song while passing a noisy percussion instrument (bells, tambourine, shaker, etc.) around the circle. At the end of the song, all children in the circle should hide their hands (and the instrument), while the child in the centre tries to guess who has the instrument. Two or three guesses should be enough. Then, with a new child in the centre, the game begins again. There are no real prizes for guessing correctly, as this should just be fun. This game also promotes the ensemble skills of working together, taking turns, treating instruments appropriately, and quietly and patiently waiting in silence while someone is guessing.

☐ Listen out

• Really work your group to maintain the singing nicely at whatever volume. This will be a challenge, but worth it!

• As this song contains only two notes, it's a good one not only for reinforcing a singing sound but also for matching pitch, especially for young singers finding this a challenge.

• Repetition! Sing the song many times, and when you repeat it think about changing the starting note up and down.

☐ Performing

• This is not a performance piece, but after it's well learned it's a great piece to use for that 'odd' few minutes in the day when either your group needs a short break or you have just finished an activity and there isn't enough time to begin something else. Those times are really valuable for preparation, practice, and skill building. Use them!

15 Cupboard key

J = 88

F

Trad. American

I have lost the cup-board key somewhere in the class-room,

Help me find the cup-board key, help me find it now.

Xylophone/boomwhacker

F major

G major

C major

D major

16 I see the moon

RESOURCES ▶ CD track 19

Information

This pretty song explores the concept of 'blessing'—that there is something greater than ourselves looking over us, and that we take care of each other. It uses only the three notes of a tonic triad (doh, me, so/1, 3, 5) and I have suggested an arrangement in two parts, and some optional tuned percussion to give a fuller texture.

Teaching and rehearsing

- The basic tune is bars 25–32 (Part 1), so start with this.

I see the moon and the moon sees me,

God bless the moon and_ God bless me.

- Gradually add the hand signs for each note. I suggest using both hands, as this will be an easier movement for this age group. Echo-sing slowly, adding the so/5 hand sign only for 'moon sees me'; then stay on verse 1 and this time add both the so/5 hand sign and the doh/1 hand sign for 'God bless me'.
- It's enough for younger singers to add just these two hand signs. When your group is confident with these you can add them all. In the first instance, just use them as motions that echo the direction of the melody. They don't necessarily need to know about sight-singing at this stage but it will prepare them for that later.
- This melody works well in two-part canon, with the second voice beginning after bar 2.

- Next learn the tune in bars 17–23.

I see the moon.____

This is a way to make the song a bit longer and will prepare the optional descant part. Again, hand signs can be helpful.
- It's never too early to encourage a group to watch a conductor. You don't have to do anything too fancy. Just indicate where to start and stop, and the tempo.

Listen out

- Or 'watch out'. When you make music of any kind, there must be a connection to the brain and the heart. For me, you can see this through the eyes of the performers. All of us have had times where music touches us. These times for me are very often not 'perfect' performances but fleeting moments that happen in the classroom when you see that connection, even for a brief moment. Watch for these and encourage them.

Performing

- Teaming this piece with the 'Two night-time songs' makes a good set in a winter holiday programme.
- If you have some young descant recorder players, try doing the descant on the recorder for some verses to add some variety.
- The introduction could be done as a solo or small group piece if you have a brave young singer/some brave young singers.

16 I see the moon

Denise Bacon
arr. Jo McNally

I see the

moon and the moon sees me,

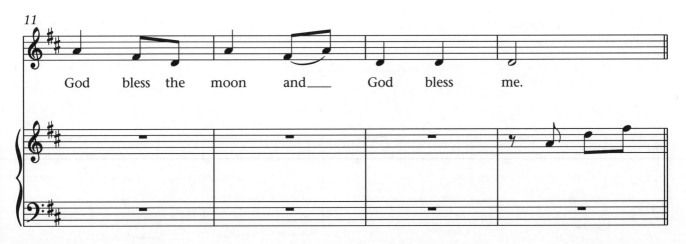

God bless the moon and___ God bless me.

God bless the moon and___ God bless me.
God bless the sun and___ God bless me.
God bless the stars and___ God bless me.

I see the moon._____
I see the sun._____
I see the stars._____

God bless me,

rit.

dim.

God bless me.

dim.

17 Ebeneezer Sneezer

RESOURCES ▶ CD track 20

▣ Information

This is one of my favourite first octave songs. The text is particularly silly and my young singers have a hard time not giggling through it. It's one of the songs they most enjoy singing. Each phrase is one note higher than the last, gradually going up the scale and then very quickly back down—a fun way to gently stretch the beginner's range.

▣ Starting

- This piece works best with a very simple accompaniment—guitar or tuned percussion—keeping a steady pulse. Introduce this as a 'silly' song. I often tell my group that the words are pretty silly and to try to echo-sing them without laughing. This works for two reasons: it sets up a sense of a challenge, and it develops listening and concentration skills.
- Sing the song for your students, or echo-sing the song phrase by phrase for them. Repeat this over several sessions until they can sing along with you. Young singers may find it difficult to sing the complete octave, but this song will help to prepare their inner ear.

▣ Teaching and rehearsing

- Using a tuned percussion instrument (bass or alto xylophone/metalophone), play four beats on C, then sing together the first bar; then play four Ds and sing the next bar, and so on.

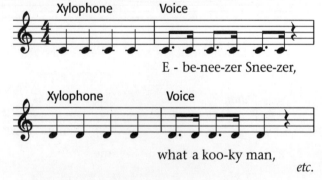

E - be-nee-zer Snee-zer,

what a koo-ky man, *etc.*

- Do the reverse of the above: start by singing each phrase, then play four beats.

- Now extend each phrase by stretching the final sound while the four beats are played.

E - be-nee-zer Snee-zer

▣ Ideas

- This song can be done in a canon starting at *, but young singers will find this difficult. Try transferring the second part to tuned percussion, substituting steady crotchets/quarter notes for the skipping rhythm of the tune.
- Most of this age group won't be able to sight-sing the full octave with confidence and understanding, but it will help them if you use hand signs like choreography as you go up the scale. Use both hands! Using hand signs in the downward scale will be difficult, but try showing the pitch direction by bringing the hands down quickly.

▣ Listen out

- Matching pitch throughout the octave will be difficult for this age group, especially since most of this song is in an upward direction—even experienced singers find this difficult. Again, posture is the key. Continually check their posture and make sure that the text is alive and active.
- Tell the story with your eyes, face, and brain. It's the connection between the text and the brain that's important; not just working on autopilot, but active storytelling.

▣ Performing

- As this is a fun song, don't try to make it too complicated. Just sing the song with guitar and percussion and add a second verse in two parts, echo-singing phrase by phrase. For older groups, try adding a verse in a round!

17 Ebeneezer Sneezer

Anon.

♩ = 138

E - be-nee - zer Snee-zer,   what   a koo - ky man,   walks up-on   his el - bows

ev - 'ry chance he can,   dress - es up   in pa - per   e - ven when   it pours,

whis-tles 'Yan-kee Doo-dle'   ev-'ry time he snores.   Oh,   E - be-nee-zer what a man! *clap Yeah!*

Tuned percussion

C   C   C   C   D   *sim.*

18 Two night-time songs

RESOURCES ▶ CD track 21

Information

These very pretty pentatonic songs are about the stars and the moon. 'Star light' is a traditional rhyme, while 'Deta' (moon) is from a Japanese folk-song. This simple but effective arrangement will help your singers to develop a beautiful singing sound.

Starting

- Don't worry about adding all the elements in the arrangement; just think of these as two separate songs (as on p. 49). Teach them over several sessions and take your time, don't rush!
- As these songs have a very calm nature, be careful when you plan to teach them. If you've just done an energetic activity and your group is ready for a rest, this could be a good time. But if they've been sitting for a while, doing a fairly intense activity, you might want to save these for later.
- For both songs, start with some gentle stretching.

Teaching and rehearsing

Star light

- Begin by echo-singing bar by bar, with hand signs. Sing clearly, quietly, and unaccompanied.
- When doing the hand signs, use both hands to reinforce and stabilize the movements. When the group is ready, inner-hear the song while doing the hand signs.
- Next add the triangle part. Use any 'sparkling' sound to start each phrase, and experiment with whatever instruments you have to hand. An octave glissando c–c' on a glockenspiel can be very effective. What do stars sound like?

Deta

- Next teach 'Deta' by rote. A guitar accompaniment works well when teaching this song, just to provide a gentle basis to maintain the pitch. Again, work phrase by phrase, carefully having the group echo each phrase accurately.
- Just enjoy the basic tune for several sessions before attempting the arrangement.
- When adding the 'I wish' for the first time, just say the words quietly instead of singing them. This may be enough of a challenge for your youngest singers. Remember, a step at a time; little victories!
- Stretch the vowel in 'wish' so the pitch will be clear and the 'sh' very quiet.

Ideas

Bells

- Singing the bell part in the arrangement is optional, but sing only the top part even when playing the two-part bell section.
- The bell part can be played in several ways:
  - Try it with individually held tone bars, one person per note.
  - Play on a xylophone or transfer to older students playing on the recorder.
  - When singing the top line of the bell part, choose either the 'so/me' or the '5/3' version, not both, and use hand signs.

Listen out

- Be very careful with the pitch in these pieces, especially the tune at 'have the wish I wish tonight'.

- Make sure that the text is very clear and sung with a smooth, legato feel.
- Make sure that breaths are not audible.
- Keep checking posture. Check your posture as well, and your singers will mimic you!

Performing

Feel free to mix and match the various components in this arrangement. Here are some suggestions:

Version I: 'Star light'
- Sing the song with the piano accompaniment and triangle part (without the bell part).
- Repeat the song, hand signing the tune while singing it.

Version II: 'Deta'
- Sing with guitar accompaniment (with or without the 'I wish' descant).

Version III: arrangement
- Start with the piano introduction and bell part (without singing).
- Sing 'Star light' with the triangle part.
- Play the bells in two parts (again without singing).
- Sing verse 1 of 'Deta' without the 'I wish' descant.
- Sing verse 2 of 'Deta' with the 'I wish' descant.
- Sing and play the bell part, then sing together the final 'I wish'.

18 Two night-time songs

Star light

Trad.

Star light, star bright, first star I see to-night, wish I may, wish I might, have the wish I wish to-night.

Deta

Trad. Japanese

1. De - ta, de - ta, in the night, with a yel-low, with a yel-low,
2. De - ta, de - ta, please don't go, will you take me with you I would

with a yel - low light, how I love to see you shine to - night.
like to fly you know, up a - bove the trees to fly, we'll go.

arrangement overleaf

This page may be photocopied

18 Two night-time songs

Trad.
arr. Jo McNally

With wonder ♩ = 90–95

so me so me doh la so so so
5 3 5 3 1 6 5 5 5

Star light, star bright, first star I see to-night, wish I may, wish I might, have the wish I wish to-night.

so me so me doh la so so so
5 3 5 3 1 6 5 5 5

This page may be photocopied

This page may be photocopied

19 Rabbits

◻ Information

This arrangement consists of two songs—'Rabbit run' and 'Old Mr Rabbit'—and a 'veggie' chant. 'Rabbit run' is a classic call-and-response song with variations for developing listening and inner-hearing skills, and 'Old Mr Rabbit' is simply an enjoyable pentatonic tune. Combining the songs with the chant provides lots of options for introducing two-part singing and a variety of performance possibilities.

◻ Teaching and rehearsing

Take your time—these are three different pieces. Don't try to teach them all in one session.

Old Mr Rabbit

- Sing the whole song for the group a couple of times. Now invite your group to give you suggestions for the type of food a rabbit might like (carrots, lettuce, chocolate). They'll probably come up with some unusual foods, but go with it! Change the ending each time and encourage them to join in:

eat-ing all my peas.—

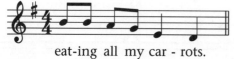

eat-ing all my car-rots.

eat-ing all my as-pa-ra-gus.

- Now extend this song with the veggie chant.

Veggie chant and improvisation

- Don't worry about teaching the written part. Start by naming some vegetables. If you have any pictures of vegetables (or any other foods), ask your group to identify them. For older groups you could use just the words instead of the pictures, developing their reading vocabulary.
- Improvise a veggie chant. Most schools have access to a small keyboard which has a backing percussion option. Explore some of the rhythms and pick a backing rhythm. You'll know a good one when the group starts

to move but is still manageable. Have fun! If you have pictures or a chart or poster of food items, point to one on the first beat of each bar, gradually making a sequence of food words.

- When your group is ready, formalize this pattern into the veggie chant of the piece or use their own ideas.
- 'Yummy' versus 'yucky'. When you teach the veggie chant you have a choice to make at the end of the piece. It would be unfair to tell you my personal preference, but suffice it to say that some foods take a while to learn to love. Let your group choose!
- Now add the 'Old Mr Rabbit' song, alternating between the veggie chant and the song.

Rabbit run

- This song is pretty straightforward. It's a basic call-and-response song, but teach it all first without making this differentiation. Start with the second half of the song ('I caught . . . then I let him go') almost as a song in itself. Then link it with the other two sections ('Old Mr Rabbit' and the veggie chant).
- Add the first four bars ('Rabbit run . . .')
- You can now link all three pieces.

◻ Ideas

Rabbit run

- As a call-and-response song, one group or solo sings the first bar, and another group sings the words in brackets. To prepare for and extend this, start with everyone singing both parts, but vary the dynamic (call: loud, response: quiet). To extend this even further, inner-hear one part then sing the other part out loud.

Old Mr Rabbit

- Change the text to rhythm syllables (ta, ti-ti/slug, spi-der)

◻ Listen out

- Each of these pieces has a unique character and style. Try to make a real difference between them.
- Keep the text very clear and clean, especially in the veggie chant.
- Young singers will enjoy the 'uh-huh', but be careful to maintain the pitch.

Performing

- Each song works individually as a short piece, but together they make a nice addition to a Spring programme or an alternative Harvest or Thanksgiving song (OK, perhaps change the Rabbit to a Turkey?!).

- The combination of the veggie chant and 'Rabbit run' is, of course, optional, depending on the abilities of your group. This could easily be done with two or more groups joining together.
- Enjoy!

19 Rabbits

Trad.
arr. Jo McNally

Rabbit run

Rab-bit run on the fro-zen ground (Who told you so?)

Rab-bit run on the fro-zen ground (How do you know?) I caught a rab-bit (Uh-huh!)

I caught a rab-bit (Uh-huh!) I caught a rab-bit (Uh-huh!) Then I let him go. *Oh!*

This page may be photocopied

Old Mr Rabbit

Veggie chant

This page may be photocopied

© Oxford University Press 2006

This page may be photocopied

20 Sweep away

RESOURCES ▶ CD track 23

☐ Information

'Sweep away', or 'The turtle will talk it seems', is a North American folk-song about dreams. In some cultures, the turtle represents the planet earth and being aware of all the things around us. If you watch them, turtles seem to look at everything. They don't appear to make a lot of sound (actually, some do, from hissing, guiro-type sounds to squawking, but the perception is that they don't); they open their mouths, but we don't often hear what they have to say. This song has a beautiful tune, with lovely stretched phrases alternating with a gentle percussion 'turtle/secret conversation'. The addition of a simple descant, sandblocks, and a rainstick make this piece thoughtful and atmospheric, and the 'conversation' can be a great start for developing the imagination and extending listening skills.

☐ Teaching and rehearsing

- If you can, start with the piano accompaniment (or play the recording). Have your group close their eyes and listen to the music. Ask them how it makes them feel. What does it sound like? Sad, happy, playful, sleepy, awake? Try this a couple of times, keeping the group calm and focused.
- With your group echoing, speak the poem quietly in rhythm. What might a turtle say? It might be a secret. What kind of a secret?
- Say the poem together, whispering, but in rhythm.
- Introduce the tune, and sing it all the way through first before echoing by phrase. The suggested breathing places are marked with a ✔. There is one optional breath where the phrase may initially be too long, but it's something to work towards.
- Add the 'turtle/secret conversation' next. This is like talking in a secret code which is completely improvised, using body percussion. Don't try to make this a rhythmic exercise. At first you ask the questions, and they make up an answer. Explore all the sounds palms together can make—clapping quietly, sliding, long slides, rhythmic slides, etc.—but reinforce that these are quiet sounds. The freer form will feel more magical (and promote listening skills). I've included a rhythmic percussion bridge for these 'conversations' which works well as a transition between the secret conversations and repeat of the tune.

☐ Ideas

- When you're ready, transfer the 'conversation' to percussion instruments. Sandblocks have a quiet, crisp sound and almost a whisper quality. If you don't have sandblocks, use palms of hands sliding across each other.
- Try xylophones or metalophones. You could start by using only one note for each 'speaker', and then work up to a pentatonic scale or even a full octave as they become more accustomed to having 'musical conversations'. Gradually add more sound options—not too many at first.

☐ Listen out

- This is a great opportunity to reinforce expressive speech. When saying the poem, explore whispering. A quiet and true whisper can be heard only by someone nearby, but a stage whisper can be heard throughout a room, especially when there is clear diction. Try both. Also, speaking in unison is a skill, and if not done carefully can sound monotone and unexpressive.
- When singing, keep the style legato and smooth. As this tune is quite challenging, with more than an octave range, take the time to work on each phrase carefully and quietly. Quiet singing will help your group to begin listening to one another and reinforce matching pitch.

☐ Performing

This works well as a performance piece. There are several options:
- Just sing the song, adding the sandblocks and descant on the repeat.
- To extend a performance:
  ○ Start with a rainstick.
  ○ Add the poem, whispered.
  ○ Sing the song with the optional descant.
  ○ Add a 'conversation'.
  ○ Repeat the song, and end with just the rainstick.

20 Sweep away

Trad. American
arr. Jo McNally

Sweep, sweep, sweep a - way, Sweep the road of dreams. Peo-ple say that in the

night, The tur-tle will talk it seems, The tur-tle will talk it seems.

Riffs

Descant recorder

Sandblocks

'Secret conversation' bridge

(play very quietly)

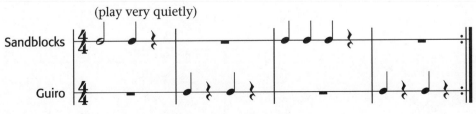

Sandblocks

Guiro

This page may be photocopied

21 You'll sing a song

▢ Information

'You'll sing a song and I'll sing a song, Then we'll sing a song together.' It sounds like a preamble to why we teach! Ella Jenkins is a music educator's treasure for singers of all ages, and this is one of my favourite songs. Her songs almost teach themselves, and I've never had a group not enjoy singing them. This one has an easy tune.

▢ Teaching and rehearsing

- Teach this song either unaccompanied or with guitar.
- The basic outline of the song is simple: 'You'll . . . I'll . . ., Then we'll . . .', introducing simple contractions.
- Each verse has two parts: the text, then the tune repeated singing on a sound, syllable, vowel, or whatever is appropriate.
- Sing each phrase separately and then have your group echo. Sing the verse and on the repeat sing it on the syllable 'la' (this really works the tongue!).
- Another way to start is to sing the first few verses and then encourage the group to join in on the repeated sound. Young singers love to make sounds that 'taste' good.

▢ Ideas

- This is a great song to continue exploring all the vocal sounds you can make, such as whispering, humming, whistling, laughing, and even clicking your tongue in rhythm.
- Try exploring vowel sounds using a smooth and even tone. This will be a challenge as your singers will need to discover where to take a breath.

- Exploring consonant sounds can also be a challenge. Some sounds, like 'm' and 'n', give a smooth sound, while others like 'b' and 'g' are more percussive. Then there are sounds like 't', 'k', and 'h' which can be rhythmic but not melodic!
- When the singing is confident, divide your group in two and sing the song as a call and response:

    Group 1: You'll sing a song
    Group 2: and I'll sing a song,
    Together: Then we'll sing a song together.
    Group 1: You'll sing a song
    Group 2: and I'll sing a song,
    Together: In warm or wintry weather.

▢ Listen out

- Try singing this song with a light vocal sound on the verse, and don't be too worried about the repeats. This is supposed to be fun!
- Watch out for the second phrase, 'Then we'll sing a song together', as this line goes up. Just keep it light and maintain good posture.

▢ Performing

- With this song, sing any time, anywhere! It works well with the whole school singing, or at a concert with the audience joining in.
- Don't forget to encourage singing on school trips, on the coach, while walking or hiking—anywhere!

21 You'll sing a song

Words and music by
Ella Jenkins

1. You'll sing a song and I'll sing a song, Then we'll sing a song to - geth - er.
   la la la la la, *etc.*

You'll sing a song and I'll sing a song, In warm or win - try wea - ther.

2. You'll clap along and I'll clap along,
   Then we'll clap along together.
   You'll clap along and I'll clap along,
   In warm or wintry weather.

   (clap)

3. You'll hum a line and I'll hum a line,
   Then we'll hum a line together,
   You'll hum a line and I'll hum a line,
   In warm or wintry weather.

   (hum)

4. You'll whistle a while and I'll whistle a while,
   Then we'll whistle a while together.
   You'll whistle a while and I'll whistle a while,
   In warm or wintry weather.

   (whistle)

Songs from Many Cultures

22 Two welcome songs

RESOURCES ▶ CD tracks 25 (Tena koe) and 26 (Sorida)

▣ Information

Here are two joyful welcome songs from New Zealand and Zimbabwe. 'Tena koe' is not strictly a traditional Maori song, but it gives a flavour of the language. 'Sorida', a song in the Shona language from Zimbabwe, combines the notes of the tonic major triad with a hand game. These songs are both a little unusual, but are great fun to sing.

▣ Starting

- Before you sing these songs, listen to the pronunciation on the CD. You'll need to make sure you are comfortable with the sounds before you try to teach the songs. Just remember to enjoy the 'taste' of the words, and your young singers will too.
- Maori vowels are have the same sound as Italian vowels. There are no real diphthongs, but many words (such as 'haere mai') have vowels sung quickly together. The text for 'Tena koe' is pronounced as follows:

Tena koe, hello to one,	*te - na* (as in f<u>a</u>r) *ko* (as in h<u>o</u>t)
	- e (as in g<u>e</u>t)
Tena **kourua**, hello to two,	*kou* (as in h<u>o</u>t) - *rua* (as *rooaa*)
Tena **koutou**, hello to all,	*ko* (as in h<u>o</u>t) - *to* (as in h<u>o</u>t)
Haere mai everyone.	*ha* (as in <u>a</u>bout)
	- e (as in <u>e</u>nter)
	- re (as in <u>e</u>nter)
	mai (*a* as in <u>a</u>bout + *ee*)

▣ Teaching and rehearsing

Tena koe

- Start with the last two phrases ('Haere mai everyone, Welcome everyone') and use as a 'good morning' call and response (Maori followed by English, or the reverse). Then add the first three phrases in the same way (Maori first).
- Sing the whole song together.
- Inner-hear the Maori part and sing the English sections out loud, then reverse.
- Sing the whole song as a call and response. Once the song is learnt, there may even be someone brave enough to sing one part as a solo or in a small group.

Sorida

- This song is satisfyingly easy to teach. Rote-sing with the hand movements phrase by phrase and have the group echo. Do this several times, always remembering to do the hand movements. The beauty of this song is that each hand movement relates to the word/syllable you're singing.
- Just singing the song can be enough of a challenge for younger singers, but have a go with partners. I introduce partner games by choosing a singer to work with me, and we show the whole game while the group sings and practises their hand patterns (many will already be joining in with someone nearby before you finish). Now everyone should try the patterns. If someone should end up without a partner, this isn't a problem as the song is short and they can work on their own until the next time. I ask my groups to change partners each time we sing the song, counting down from ten to limit the time it takes to find a new partner!
- I've also introduced this song to older singers, and it is suitable for singers of any age.
- This piece also works well as a round, starting at *.

▣ Ideas

- Many schools these days have multicultural student populations and there will often be a 'welcome' sign near the school entrance in the languages represented in the school. Learning to say 'hello and welcome' can be a great way of sharing cultures and languages.
- Both pieces provide useful repertoire for all age groups.

▣ Listen out

- Take your time with these pieces, and don't be put off by non-English texts. While it is important to be accurate while singing songs from other cultures, this shouldn't spoil your enjoyment of the songs.

▣ Performing

- Both pieces could be used as a set for performance, but a better way to use them may be to combine phrases of welcome in all the cultures represented within your school, interspersed with several welcome songs (including 'Fun mje alafia', p. 32), perhaps as the opening to a school concert.
- Include them as part of a 'parents' evening'—and yes, get the parents to sing them as well!
- Make the pieces in this section part of a project for the whole school and have everyone learn the welcome songs.
- Use any of the pieces at the start of an assembly, or as a greeting to a visitor.

22 Two welcome songs

Tena koe

Trad.

♩ = 84

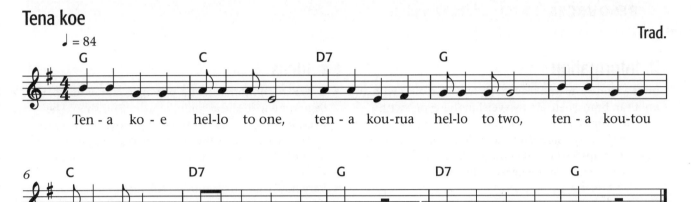

Ten - a ko - e hel-lo to one, ten - a kou-rua hel-lo to two, ten - a kou-tou

hel-lo to all, hae-re mai ev - ery - one, wel-come ev - ery - one.

Sorida

Trad. Zimbabwean

♩. = 44

circle   *clap*   *circle*   *clap*   *back of hands*   *back of hands*

So - ri - da   So - ri - da   ri - da   ri - da

right   *left together*   *right*   *left together*   *back of hands*   *back of hands*

da   da da   da   da da   ri - da   ri - da.

Hand claps

Key

1. So - ri - da   make a circle out to the side with both hands, finishing with a clap on 'da'.

2. ri - da ri - da   touch back of hands to back of partner's hands on each syllable.

3. da da da   touch partner's right forearm; touch partner's left forearm; clap hands together.

This page may be photocopied

23 White banana (Barbados)

RESOURCES ▶ CD tracks 27 and 28

☐ Information

This is a wonderful and lively song from Barbados with a Caribbean beat. There are two versions here: one with guitar and optional percussion, and the other an extended arrangement with piano and percussion. This song is fun to sing, perhaps at the end of the week, and it really gets the body feeling and moving with the music.

☐ Starting

- There are two ways to approach this song: either speak the text rhythmically or just dive into the melody. Either will work, so long as the approach has energy and 'attitude'.
- Start with the first four bars. Say or sing the words to your group in rhythm, including the claps. Putting a movement in these rests will help to keep this rhythm accurate.
- Keep the diction crisp, clean, and with plenty of 'attitude'.
- Now sing the phrase with the group echoing each bar, and then sing the whole phrase together.
- Follow the same process with each four-bar phrase.

Percussion

- There are two percussion accompaniments for this song, both using the same instruments. The first, used in the arrangement, is the most suitable for this age group, while the second is more complex. Both are based on keeping a steady pulse. Don't try to add all the instruments in your first session!
- When using the first set of parts, count the four beats 1, 2, 3, 4, then gradually add the instruments. Pat alternate knees with the maracas, and have your conga and cowbell/clave players say 'sh' with hands apart in the rests.
- Think of the percussion parts as belonging to a selection of repertoire patterns that can then be used to accompany other songs. Once a pattern (rhythmic or melodic) is learned, re-using it will help your group to develop aural memory and can lead to developing music-reading skills.

☐ Ideas

- If you are comfortable with playing guitar or piano, try beginning with the accompaniment. This should be lively and happy, and let the group move to the music. To keep your singers listening and focused, get them to 'freeze' when the music stops. Do this several times as a game.
- Vary how your group moves. The main rule is that no one touches anyone else!
  - ○ Sitting down, move a specific body part (head, shoulders, arms, face, etc.).
  - ○ Standing, move anything except the feet (keeping balance could be a challenge).
  - ○ Standing, move everything, but stay in place.
  - ○ Move to the music around the room, not touching anyone else and keeping the space 'looking full'. This keeps the children focused not only on their own movement but on the spacing of the group, so that everyone is moving safely.
- This would be a great piece to come back to in future years, for developing sight-singing and rhythm-reading skills.

☐ Performing

Both versions work well as performance pieces, but the best thing about all the songs in this section is that they can be sung anywhere. Always try to include singing as part of your day. It doesn't always have to be beautiful, but it should be natural and joyous.

- Sing the song with guitar and add any or all of percussion set 1.
- The arrangement starts with a percussion introduction, the instruments added gradually until a pattern is built up. Sing the song accompanied by percussion set 1 (shown in the score), or set 2 if your group is more able.
- The ending reverses the introduction, gradually taking out the percussion as the repeated last phrase is sung more quietly each time until the final whisper.

23 White banana (Barbados)

Trad. Barbados
arr. Jo McNally

Happily ♩ = 62

Three white hor-ses   in   the sta-ble,   Hey,   hey we go   off   to-mor-row.

Off   to-mor-row is a   break-up   day,   Come   a-long with your   shal-low plate,

shal-low plate 'tis a   white   ba-na-na,   Hey,   hey we go   off   to-mor-row.

Percussion

arrangement overleaf

Set 1

Maracas

Conga

Cowbell/Clave

Set 2

This page may be photocopied

23 White banana (Barbados)

Trad. Barbados
arr. Jo McNally

Happily ♩ = 62

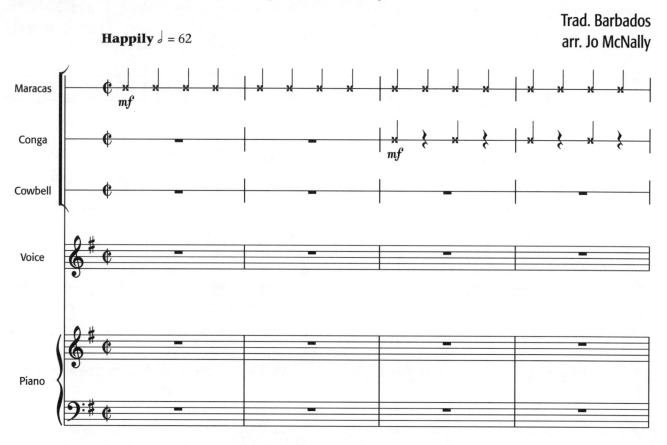

This page may be photocopied

Courtesy of *World Song Project*, published by the Camden Music Service, London Borough of Camden.

Three white hor - ses   in   the sta - ble,   Hey,   hey we go   off   to-mor-row.

Off   to-mor-row is a   break - up   day,   Come a-long with your   shal - low plate,

This page may be photocopied

Courtesy of *World Song Project*, published by the Camden Music Service, London Borough of Camden.

24 Chanda mama (India)

RESOURCES ▶ CD track 29

☐ Information

'Chanda mama' is a children's song about the moon in Hindi. It has short, repetitive phrases and a beautiful text, and I love the light and lilting quality to its tune. Enjoy singing this one unaccompanied.

☐ Starting

- Before teaching this piece, listen carefully to the CD and the pronunciation of the words.
- Look at the form of the song and listen for rhyming words, similar phrases, repeated words, and repeated tunes.

☐ Teaching and rehearsing

- Have your group listen to the CD. There might be someone in your group who knows the song. You could be surprised!
- Start with the first line, which is also the last line. Teach this one first, then listen to the CD and have the group raise their hands when they hear those words. The older end of this age group should be able to identify that this is the beginning and the end of the song. Now sing along with the CD. Repeat the same process with each new phrase, gradually adding them to the song.

☐ Ideas

- Every culture has its own children's songs, games, and rhymes, and there is a wealth of our heritage that needs to be cherished and remembered; start collecting now!
- Assign homework to collect from parents, grandparents, aunts, uncles, and friends any songs or rhymes that they can remember from their childhood. Ask each of your students to share one of these with the class—and don't forget to check your own family!

☐ Listen out

- The text is very straightforward and, unlike English text, everything here is pronounced. Make sure you don't drop the endings of words (too - t, roo - th). If the diction is used well here it will add to the rhythmic lilt of the piece.
- Start encouraging listening skills early on, not only to develop inner-hearing but to give your group the confidence to examine what they hear. This can be done with any song or piece of music, but the key is to be specific about what you're listening for.

☐ Performing

- This song would work well as part of an international festival. Just sing and enjoy.

24 Chanda mama (India)

Trad. Hindi

♩ = 74

Chan-da ma-ma doo - r ke Kho-e pa-ka-yein boo - r ke Aa - p kha-yein

tha - li mein Mu-nne ko dein pya - li mein Pya - li ga - yi too - t

Mu-nna ga - ya roo - th Na - yi pya - li li - an ghay Mu-nne ko ma -

- na-yen - ge Doodh ma-lai___ kha-yen - ge Chan-da ma-ma doo - r ke.

Uncle moon is far away
As we eat pancake from a tray.
The little boy is eating from a china bowl.
The bowl breaks,
The boy sulks.
We will buy a new one to comfort him
And he will eat his milk and cream.

25 Ali Baba (Morocco)

RESOURCES ▶ CD track 30

☐ Information

This short, lively, rhythmic, and quirky song in Arabic is often sung to very young children. Young singers will thoroughly enjoy the song and the meaning of the text!

☐ Teaching and rehearsing

- There are only two phrases, each with the same melody, so start with the tune.
- Choose a neutral syllable (la, doh) and sing the tune without the text. Alternatively, you could play the tune on an instrument. The recorder is better for demonstration than the piano because it has a clear, pure tone which relates well to vocal sound. The treble is a good choice as the timbre is closer to the human voice, but a descant will do as well.
- With your group listening carefully, play or sing the tune again, but this time ask them to raise their hands (or make another agreed movement) when they hear the tune repeat. Do this several times.
- Now sing the song, with the text complete and the optional claps. Do this several times until the group are joining in. They'll get the clapping right first and with each repetition will gradually add the text; 'Ali Baba' and 'Salah Aldien' will probably be the first words they'll pick up.
- Be patient with your group and gradually help them with the pronunciation and the text.

☐ Ideas

- Tell your group about the song, what it means, and where it's from. For slightly older singers, ask them where they think the song might be from and, from just the sound, what they think it might mean.
- Act out the story!
- As your groups gradually add to their multi-ethnic repertoire, keep track on a world map of all the places their songs come from. This makes a great all-school project.
- Try varying the number of claps between each phrase. One, two, and three work well. Try four or more at your peril!

☐ Listen out

- Work towards singing this song in two phrases with only one breath at the end of the second bar. If the dotted crotchets/quarter notes aren't held to the full length (the temptation will be to take a breath), change the clapping accompaniment to the hands palm-sliding against each other while the notes are 'stretched'. This should keep the notes to full value and the phrase complete.

☐ Performing

- This piece is best done unaccompanied or with simple percussion, perhaps using a tambourine instead of clapping. Keep it simple.
- Consider doing a programme of songs as a trip around the world.

25 Ali Baba (Morocco)

Trad. Morocco

A - li   Ba - ba   rai - ess   Al - es - aa - ba   Sal -

-ah   Al - dien   Mask - out   Al - wa - lie - dieen.

A man had a farm.
He worked day and night,
But whenever he began to work
He fell asleep.

This page may be photocopied

26 Oranges and lemons (England)

☐ Information

In and around London are many churches with many bells. Bells have been used to celebrate holidays and special national events, and even to pass a warning. 'Oranges and lemons' is a well-known traditional rhyme, the text of which dates back to the middle of the sixteenth century. Paul Ayres is a skilful British composer who writes wonderfully for choirs at all levels of development, and his work is a joy to sing. His arrangement is for young choirs and includes the basic elements of a traditional poem, a chant, and a 'bell' accompaniment. Don't be put off by a first look. This is a piece to keep returning to over several years, gradually adding and improving each section, and it will become a useful addition to any young choir's repertoire. I have also included a simpler version of the song, with guitar chords.

☐ Teaching and rehearsing

- There are three sections to this piece:

  1. traditional song ('Oranges and lemons')
  2. chant ('Here comes a candle')
  3. bells ('Ding dong bell')

  For this level begin with the three sections individually, not the arrangement.

Oranges and lemons

- This poem is built on quasi-rhyming words, so begin with these and just say each phrase with your group repeating it:

  lemons/St Clement's
  farthings/St Martin's
  pay me/Old Bailey
  grow rich/Shoreditch
  that be/Stepney
  know/Bow

  Do this several times, until they can guess the church name:

  Leader: Oranges and lemons, say the bells of . . .
  Group: St Clements.
  Leader: I owe you five farthings, say the bells of . . .
  Group: St Martin's.
  and so on.

- Now teach the melody. The song is quite simple if you take care over the beginnings of each phrase. Just make sure that you begin on the correct pitch (C, G, or F), as this will be very difficult to fix after the group has learnt

the song. Show the three pitches with any type of hand sign. This is a good opportunity to prepare so, me, and doh.

Here comes a candle (optional if too scary or too violent for your group)

- The text reads like a nightmare, comforting in the first phrase ('light you to bed') but scary in the second phrase ('chop off your head'). Learn the text with clear diction.
- Vary the quality of the sound (angry, scary, spooky, happy).
- Vary the dynamics for each phrase (loud/soft, soft/loud, gradually louder/softer) and find out which your group likes best.
- Slightly older groups can do the text in a two- or three-part canon starting at *, but remember to include dynamic changes.

Ding dong bell

- For this age group, transfer this part to a glockenspiel or bells using only the notes F, A, and C in any octave, and use as an introduction to the song.
- Discuss church bells and how they sound, ringing and chiming the hour. The ringing might be an elaborate mixture of pitches, often in a repeated pattern, but chimes on the hour are usually on a repeated tone. Improvise a ringing pattern followed by a chiming pattern on any combination of F, A, and C.
- When you have an improvisation you like, write a score with the letters in the order in which they should be played (a simple composing exercise!).

☐ Ideas

- Listen to the bells where you live and work. Does your school use bells to mark certain times of the school day? Are the students lined up to a bell, whistle, or something else? Can you hear the bells of a nearby church, and do they ring or chime during the day or only on Sunday?
- Try being the 'bells' of your school for a day (or part of a day).
- Use your building to pass a message by bells and song. Position two or three small teams in several places in the school, within listening distance of each other. Group 1 plays their improvisation and then starts singing the song. Group 2 begins to play and sing when they hear the first group finish, then Group 3 takes over when Group 2 has finished, and so on.

- There's also a game associated with this song, played a bit like 'London Bridge'. Two players make an arch while the others file under it, walking in a circle. At the end of the song, on the word 'head', the 'arch' is lowered and the player underneath it is trapped and must choose 'oranges or lemons'. Keep singing and playing until the entire group is divided in two, then have a 'tug of war'. This could be a good way to randomly divide your group for their next activity.

▣ Listen out

- Traditionally, there are no breaks or rests between each phrase of the melody, but in Paul's arrangement some of the phrases are separated by one or two bars' rest. These need to be very clear for the arrangement to work correctly. Put some space between each phrase and consider getting the group to respond to a start/stop conducting gesture. Sing the song (without the 'bell' accompaniment) and vary by hand gestures the time between phrases.

▣ Performing

- Paul's arrangement works well and will be a good part of any beginning choir repertoire, but this age group may need the simpler version, with all the elements separated.
- The simplest version is to do the bell part or improvisation as an introduction, sing the song, and then say the poem.
- To extend this, incorporate the team version of the bell improvisation by placing one team for each of the six churches about the performance space. Then each team in turn plays their improvisation and sings the line of text for their church. A good way to finish each phrase would be to chime the hour, with each team chiming one hour later. When all the teams have finished, do the chant together (or in canon) from their places about the room, making it very atmospheric!

26 Oranges and lemons (England)

Song

Trad. English

♩. = 54

O-ran-ges and le-mons, say the bells of St Cle-ment's. You owe me five

far-things, say the bells of St Mar-tin's. When will you pay me? say the

bells of Old Bai-ley. When I grow rich, say the bells of Shore-ditch. When will that

be? say the bells of Step - ney. I do not know, says the great bell of Bow.

Bells/glockenspiel introduction

(Ding dong bell)

Chant

Here comes a can-dle to light you to bed.   Here comes a chop-per to chop off your head.

© Oxford University Press 2006

26   Oranges and lemons (England)

Trad. English
arr. Paul Ayres

One in a bar ♩ = 46

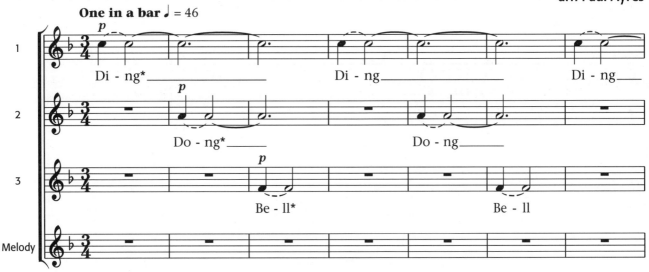

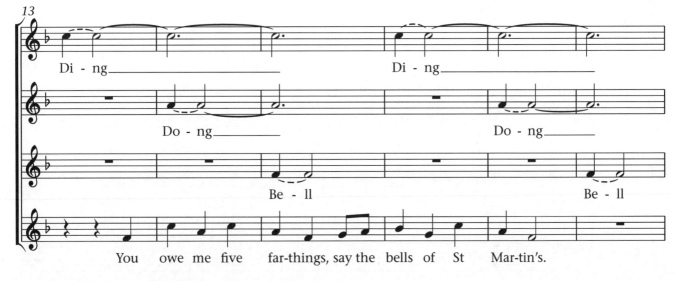

* Close the vowel sound on the second crotchet.

This page may be photocopied

This page may be photocopied

27 Hotaru koi (Japan)

RESOURCES ▶ CD track 33 (arrangement p. 82)

☐ Information

Fireflies, or lightning bugs, are one of the most beautiful and wonderful sights on a summer evening, like small dots of 'fairy lights' hovering over a garden. This is a very accessible Japanese song with lots of repetition and only four different notes. It is suitable not only for young singers but also for young recorder players, and when sung in a round has a lovely effect of fireflies sparkling. I have included the basic song with some added percussion which is great for this age group, and the more formal arrangement works well for young beginning choirs.

☐ Teaching and rehearsing

- There are four lines of text, and the last line is a repeat of the first. Lines two and three have the same melody but the text is slightly different, so the form is ABCA:

      A   Ho, ho, hotaru koi,
      B   atchi no mizu wa nigai zo,
      C   kotchi no mizu wa amai zo,
      A   ho, ho, hotaru koi.

- Start with 'Ho, ho, hotaru koi'. Sing this quietly to the group several times with them repeating it each time.
- Tell your group that this song is from Japan and is about a firefly or lightning bug. Find out if any of the group have ever seen them.
- Now look at the second and third lines. Notice that there are strong similarities, but more importantly occasional differences. When learning these lines, give the highlighted text a little extra stress. You'll need to repeat these carefully several times.

      B   **at**chi no mizu wa **nig**ai zo
      C   **kot**chi no mizu wa **am**ai zo

- Now sing the whole song, and add a triangle or finger cymbals on the words 'koi' and 'zo' to add a bit of sparkle. (Be aware when doing the arrangement that the finger cymbals part on 'koi' refers to the descant/recorder part.)
- Adding a simple ostinato is a useful way to introduce the concept of part-singing. The best choice here is the line 'Ho, ho, hotaru koi'. Have part of the group sing this line or play it on the recorder, and then continue singing or playing it while everyone else sings the tune.
- Once the tune is confident, gradually add the percussion parts.

☐ Ideas

- I often teach this song with the text written out as a poster, varying the colour of each phrase depending on the form and similarities in the text. The first and last lines should be the same colour, but lines 2 and 3 use two colours—one for syllables and words that are the same, and another for those that are different. Identifying similarities and differences can be a useful exercise in developing reading skills.
- This song is great sung as a round and is a bit unusual in that there are four places to start the round. They are listed on the score by number, with 1 the easiest and 4 the most difficult. For this age group, stay with options 1 and 2.
- It can be fun to have somewhere in the room a string of twinkling holiday lights to be the fireflies of the song.

☐ Listen out

- Really listen out for the differences between the phrases B and C. It's very easy to confuse them, especially when singing in a canon.
- Think about the quality of the sound. Keep the singing light and easy, and don't force the sound. Consider how small a firefly is—the singing should reflect this. If the song is sung too heavily it will sound like a 200 kilo bug!
- Keep a steady pulse; the bass xylophone part can be very useful for this. Especially when singing with the ostinato or in parts, tempo and pitch need to be reinforced for this age group.

☐ Performing

As a performance piece, this song works on many levels as part of an international songs programme or set of night or insect songs. There are two versions here: a simple version and a full arrangement. Of course, either version would be enhanced by twinkling holiday lights!
- Simple version:
  ○ Play the two-bar introduction on the bass xylophone, which then continues throughout the piece.
  ○ Sing the song with or without the finger cymbals/triangle part.
  ○ On the repeat, play the two-bar introduction, then start the ostinato and then add the triangle part and the song.

27 Hotaru koi (Japan)

Melody

Trad. Japanese

Ho, ho, ho - ta - ru koi, at - chi no mi - zu wa ni - ga - i zo,

ko - tchi no mi - zu wa a - ma - i zo, ho, ho, ho - tar - u koi.

Ho, ho, fireflies, come here!
That water is bitter,
This water is sweet,
Ho, ho, fireflies, come here!

Percussion

Finger cymbals/triangle

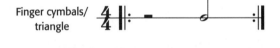

Bass xylophone

Alto xylophone

arrangement overleaf

* There are four places to start a round, 1 the easiest and 4 the most difficult.

27 Hotaru koi (Japan)

Trad. Japanese
arr. Jo McNally

© Oxford University Press 2006

Just for Fun

28 Bingo

◻ Information

'Bingo' is probably one of the best-known tunes for younger singers and can be heard on coach rides, school trips, and family outings. I always thought 'Bingo' had an American origin, but some sources suggest that it may be from the UK (specifically England or Wales). Either way, it's a great song, and usually one that adults tire of singing (and listening to) long before kids do!

◻ Teaching and rehearsing

* Make five cards, each containing a letter from the word 'Bingo'; leave the back of the cards blank.
* As the younger end of this age group will be learning their alphabet, get them to identify each letter name, eventually sounding out the word 'Bingo'. (If you would prefer not to make cards, writing the letters on a whiteboard will work just as well. I have a small one, A3 size, that I can carry with me from class to class.)
* Keep the letters showing as you rote-sing the song with your group.
* Repeat the song, and each time you sing it take away one of the spelled letters by turning over the card or rubbing out the letter on the whiteboard and clap instead of singing the letter. Repeat this until all the letters are being clapped.

etc.

◻ Ideas

* Change the animal and its name: for example, 'There was a farmer had a cat and _ _ _ _ _ was his/her name-oh'. Any animal will do, but it's useful to start with five-letter names.
* Substitute a silence instead of the 'clap', and inner-hear the letters.
* When your group can sing the song confidently, stretch them by taking off the letters backwards!

etc.

* For a very experienced group (and as a challenge for grown-ups!), take off the letters randomly:

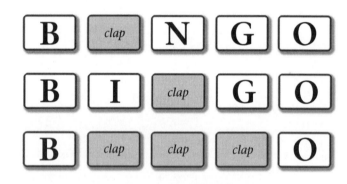

. . . and my personal favourite (although not for the very young):

clap I N G clap

◻ Listen out

* This song is quite straightforward, but take care at the beginning of each verse. Sometimes the singing can get a bit wild, so I have included an optional pause on the first word 'There'. This gives the group chance to re-group and match pitch before continuing.
* I have suggested guitar chords, but this song works just as well unaccompanied. Don't feel stuck singing in the given key, but experiment with changing the starting note. The pause at the beginning of each verse is a good opportunity to change keys.

28 Bingo

Trad.

♩ = 120

There was a far-mer had a dog and 'Bin-go' was his name - oh

B - I - N-G-O, B - I - N-G-O, B - I - N-G-O and 'Bin-go' was his name-oh.

This page may be photocopied

29 Rainy old, gloomy old day

RESOURCES   ▶ CD track 35

Information

Living in the UK as I do, one gets used to this type of day! It happens so frequently that in many schools you'll see rooms designated for 'wet play' as you walk through the corridors. I like this song. The text is simple, with many words accessible to beginning readers, and the tune is lovely. There are three verses but unusually no chorus. I have added a simple piano part, but this song also works well unaccompanied.

Teaching and rehearsing

- Take your time teaching this one. For the very youngest singers verse 1 will be enough. For slightly older singers, give them the text first and begin teaching the song as a reading exercise, identifying any words they know.
- Introduce the tune for the first phrase. Sing the first phrase and, with your group, read the rest of the first phrase and finally sing the last phrase.
- Introduce the tune for the second phrase, then repeat the song singing all the known tune but reading any of the song they don't know.
- This time introduce the third phrase, then sing the whole verse.
- Once the tune is learned, adding the other verses will be quite straightforward—but take your time.

Ideas

- Find a time to sing something with your class each day! Why not start with the weather? Here are a few weather rhymes:

    Rain, rain, go away,
    Come again another day.
    All the children want to play,
    Rain, rain, go away.

    Whether the weather is cold,
    Or whether the weather is hot,
    Whatever the weather there'll always be weather,
    Whether there's weather or not.

    Sky blue, sky blue,
    A sunny day is here for you.

    Slipping, sliding on the ice,
    Making snowmen can be nice.
    But when the sun is in the sky,
    He warms and melts, and then goodbye!

    As the days grow longer the winds grow stronger!

- Say them as poems.
- Try them as spoken rounds—the second part can enter anywhere.
- Drone-sing them on one pitch, then try as a round.
- Have a student improvise a tune.

Listen out

- Make sure that you listen to the recording if you're unsure how verses 2–3 work with the tune. Be aware that, when there is more than one verse, the rhythm of subsequent verses may alter to accommodate the text and may not be obvious at first.

29 Rainy old, gloomy old day

Words and melody by
Fran Carpenter

Sadly ♩ = 94

con Ped.

1. It's a rain-y old, gloom-y old day,
2. It's__ rain-ing and I've got to stay in!
3. It's__ rain-ing and I can't go out,

And I can't go out to play, All the
But I'd ra-ther go for a swim! To the
There are too ma-ny grown-ups a-bout! Oh,__

grown-ups in-side, They__ like to hide On a rain-y old, gloom-y old day.
pud-dles I'd dash Have a good old splash! But it's rain-ing and I've got to stay in.
what bad luck That I'm not a duck! When it's rain-ing and I can't go out.

This page may be photocopied

30 The ants go marching

RESOURCES ► CD track 36

☐ Information

This song about a little marching ant is a favourite with my classes. It's a wonderfully versatile song with ten verses featuring rhyming words. It is also a great song for encouraging small group and solo singing and for developing listening skills. I added the optional accompanied 'ant marching' because my students couldn't sit still—it's a song they just needed to move to!

☐ Teaching and rehearsing

- This is a very easy song to teach, and you don't even have to rote-sing. Just sing the song and with each verse the group will gradually join in with more of the text and tune.
- To get started, sing the first verse twice, and when you repeat it slow down and leave a space for the 'hurrah's, encouraging your group to fill in the space.
- For the next few verses, see if they can remember what the number is and fill in that blank.
- In your first few sessions sing only a few verses (five is probably enough for this age group until they become more confident).
- By this time the energy level will be rising and your group will probably need to do some moving! So begin by tapping one finger on each knee (in a steady pulse) for the first verse, gradually adding another finger for each verse. Alternatively, have two students standing marching side by side, then in each verse add two more students marching behind them, gradually adding to the line. If you're brave, let the groups march about the room while singing!

☐ Ideas

- Change the phrase with the rhyming word; let your group choose.

Basic part-singing

- This is a great song for taking turns. Divide the group in two, with some children singing the tune and the rest singing the 'hurrah's; they should all join in at 'and they all go . . .'. Swap parts for the next verse.

- Do the above, but this time substitute one of the groups (either the singing or the 'hurrah's) with a solo or small group.
- Try inner-hearing part of the song. Sing a verse but inner-hear the 'hurrah's, then reverse this. For a real challenge, inner-hear the whole song with a guitar accompaniment then sing out loud at 'and they all go . . .'.
- Try your own combinations of the above. Challenge your group and surprise one another.

Ant marching

- This is purely optional but a lot of fun. There are three basic parts:
  1. Call to attention: everyone should 'freeze' when someone—usually the group leader—plays and says the text 'Work, work', then respond '1 2 3 4!'.
  2. Marching: start by marching around the room to a steady beat while saying the 'Looking here, looking there' text, keeping the brain and body focused. Do this individually at first, then in larger groups, following in a line. Remember the rules: try to keep the space looking full and avoid contact with any other group.
  3. Search for food: when the tambourine shakes, everyone should move as an individual again, keeping the space looking full and not touching any other 'ants'.

☐ Listen out

- Be careful with the 'hurrah's: the first one goes down, while the second one goes up.
- Keep the singing fresh and fun. The group will probably enjoy this song and occasionally sing with volume and gusto, not always considering pitch. Try varying the dynamics of each verse while keeping the text clear.

30 The ants go marching

Trad.

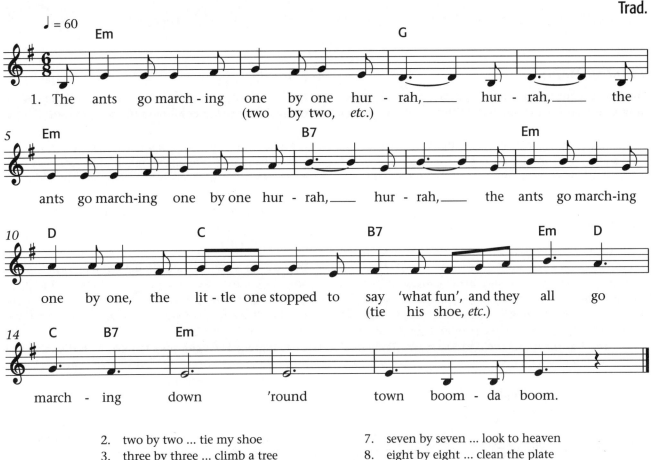

♩ = 60

1. The ants go march-ing one by one hur-rah,___ hur-rah,___ the
(two by two, *etc.*)

ants go march-ing one by one hur-rah,___ hur-rah,___ the ants go march-ing

one by one, the lit-tle one stopped to say 'what fun', and they all go
(tie his shoe, *etc.*)

march-ing down 'round town boom-da boom.

2. two by two ... tie my shoe	7. seven by seven ... look to heaven
3. three by three ... climb a tree	8. eight by eight ... clean the plate
4. four by four ... shut the door	9. nine by nine ... climb a vine
5. five by five ... learn to dive	10. ten by ten ... start again
6. six by six ... pick up sticks	

Ant marching

Call to attention

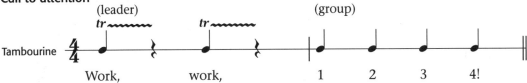

(leader)   (group)

Tambourine

Work, work, 1 2 3 4!

Marching

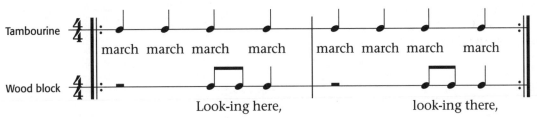

Tambourine

march march march march | march march march march

Wood block

Look-ing here, look-ing there,

Search for food

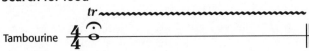

Tambourine

This page may be photocopied

31 B-A bay

RESOURCES ▶ CD track 37

◻ Information

'B-A bay' is a great alphabet song and a real tongue-twister! Each verse uses all the vowel sounds and the sounds or words they make when combined with consonants. It's great fun and good alphabet practice, and gives a good work-out for the lips, teeth, and tongue, although it's pretty silly and some of the combinations turn into strange-sounding words, so be careful!

◻ Starting

- Make sure you can sing this song confidently before teaching it—it's very important with this one! The tongue-twister aspect is quite challenging, so have a few consonants you're comfortable with for the first few times you sing the song. B, C, D, H, M, and Z are good starters; T, X, and W aren't! Be careful with the letters F, G, P, and T as the words could surprise you. Try them outside the classroom first.

◻ Teaching and rehearsing

- This is a another song to teach by rote—sing it to the group and have them echo bar by bar. Especially with this song, the repetition gets the sounds into their ears and reinforces listening skills.
- Take your time and sing each verse a couple of times; enjoy the 'taste' of the sounds.

◻ Ideas

- Once you have introduced the song to your group, let them choose which consonant to use next.
- I use this song for just about any age group. The older the group, the more consonants you can use, until you're ready for the 'alphabet marathon'—yes, trying to get through all the consonants in one session! By this time the group should know the song really well and be able to sing without repeating each line.

◻ Listen out

- Young singers will probably find it difficult to choose only the consonants, so be patient. No matter how you reinforce this—and even if you stress that all the vowels are already contained in the song—someone will always choose A, E, I, O, or U!
- As your group becomes more familiar with the song, they will begin to hear and identify that some of the sound combinations make words: b + a = bay, m + a = may, for example.

31 B-A bay

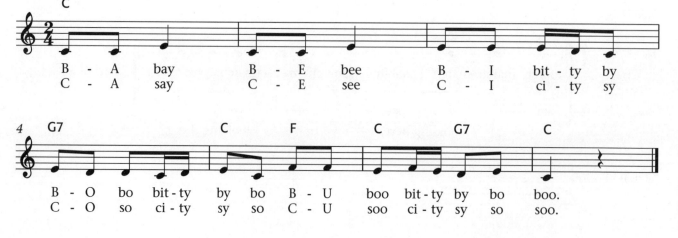

This page may be photocopied

32 Grizzly bear

RESOURCES ▶ CD track 38

☐ Information

This is a very fun song to sing about a 'gri - zz - ly' bear! Kevin Stannard's jolly arrangement challenges the singer as well as the keyboard player, and the piece creates a bridge between the repertoire in *Young Voiceworks* and the extended materials in *Junior Voiceworks*.

☐ Teaching and rehearsing

- The accompaniment is challenging, so begin with the tune unaccompanied.
- Start by echo-singing each phrase with your group. Be careful to distinguish between the ends of phrases where the tunes goes up or down. When singing the words 'going' and 'doing', move your hands upward or downward to show the shape of the phrase.
- To get a good feel for the entrances of each phrase, sing along with the CD before adding a 'live' accompaniment. This way you can show your group where they should start and stop—a basic but valuable lesson in how to follow a conductor!
- The second part beginning at bar 17 is not for this age group but would be good for older singers.

☐ Ideas

- Try varying the dynamics as you sing, perhaps gradually getting louder throughout the song.
- Explore animal sounds, especially wild animals, and add a soundscape (see p. xvi) to introduce the piece. Scary sounds would be a nice contrast to the fun feel of the song!

☐ Listen out

- Have a good look at the text and the repeated words 'ever' and 'never'. These usually appear in groups of three—with the exception of the final phrase. Be careful!
- This is also a great piece for developing good diction.

☐ Performing

- 'Grizzy bear' would be a good addition to programmes with an animal theme!

32 Grizzly bear

Words by Mary Austin
Music by Kevin Stannard

Lively ♩ = 96

If you e-ver, e-ver, e-ver meet a gri-zz-ly bear,

You must ne-ver, ne-ver, ne-ver, ask him where_____ he is go-ing.

If you e-ver, e-ver, e-ver meet a gri-zz-ly bear,

This page may be photocopied

You must ne-ver, ne-ver, ne-ver, ask him what_____ he is do-ing.

For if you e-ver, e-ver, dare to stop a gri-zz-ly bear, gri-zz-ly bear,

You will ne-ver, ne-ver, ne-ver, ne-ver, meet an-o-ther gri-zz-ly

bear.

dim. al fine

This page may be photocopied

Glossary

beat: *see* 'pulse'

call and response: sung phrases shared between a leader and a group

canon: *see* 'round'

chant: a melodic line that has a limited vocal range, perhaps only one note

drone singing: singing that remains on one pitch

dynamics: indications of different levels of sound or volume

echo singing: style of rote teaching where a leader demonstrates and the group repeats (echoes) what they hear

graphic score: using pictures or symbols to represent sound

inner-hearing: the act of hearing singing or speaking inside your head

interval: the distance between notes

matching pitch: the ability to reproduce a specific sound or pitch, both as an individual and within a group

ostinato: a short, repetitive rhythmic pattern that can be rhythmic or melodic, or both

part-singing: different vocal lines sung at the same time

pentatonic: based on the pentatonic scale—a scale consisting of five notes

pitch: the sound of notes relative to one other, high or low

question and answer: sung phrases shared between a leader and a group, or between two groups

rote: the learning of music (by ear) by repetition until secure

round (also 'canon'):   a line of music that can be sung against itself, starting at different points within the phrase

sequence: a pattern that is repeated with the starting pitch higher or lower

solo/soli: one person singing on their own, or a small group singing

soundscape/sound stories: representing a place, story, or 'real' sound using vocal or instrumental means

space management: the ability of a group to move with respect for others and for the space

syncopation: accenting or stressing weak beats in rhythm, or between main beats to produce catchy or exciting rhythms

tempo: speed

timbre: quality of sound

unison: every voice singing the same melody at the same time

vocal folds: vocal chords

vocal qualities: the variety of sounds that any voice can make (i.e. singing, speaking, whispering, making a squeaky voice, and so on)

vocal range: the variety of pitches for any given song

CD credits

The CD was recorded at St John Fisher Roman Catholic Primary School, Harrow, Middlesex, in December 2005 and February 2006.

Singers:	years 3, 5, and 6 at St John Fisher School; Jo McNally
Recording engineer:	Alan Burgess
Keyboard:	Emily Chelu; Geoff Boyd
Guitar:	Geoff Boyd; Jo McNally